The
GLORY
of GOD'S
GRACE

Also by James Montgomery Boice

Christ's Call to Discipleship
The Minor Prophets
Ordinary Men Called by God
Standing on the Rock

The GLORY of GOD'S GRACE

The Meaning of God's Grace—
and How It Can Change Your Life

JAMES MONTGOMERY BOICE

kregel
PUBLICATIONS

Grand Rapids, MI 49501

The Glory of God's Grace: The Meaning of God's Grace—and How It Can Change Your Life

Copyright © 1993 by James Montgomery Boice

Published in 1999 by Kregel Publications, a division of Kregel, Inc., P.O. Box 2607, Grand Rapids, MI 49501. Kregel Publications provides trusted, biblical publications for Christian growth and service. Your comments and suggestions are valued.

For more information about Kregel Publications, visit our web site at www.kregel.com.

Cover design: Frank Gutbrod
Cover photo: © PhotoDisc

Library of Congress Cataloging-in-Publication Data
Boice, James Montgomery.
  [Amazing grace]
  The glory of God's grace: the meaning of God's grace—and how it can change your life / by James Montgomery Boice.
    p.   cm.
  Originally published: Amazing Grace. Wheaton, Ill.: Tyndale House Publishers ©1993.
Includes indexes.
  1. Grace (Theology). NT I. Title.
BT761.2.B65   1999   234—dc 21   99-18854
                                 CIP

ISBN 0-8254-2072-5

Printed in the United States of America

1 2 3 4 5 / 03 02 01 00 99

TO HIM
who is able to make all grace abound to you,
so that in all things at all times,
having all that you need,
you will abound in every good work

CONTENTS

PREFACE

Amazing grace! how sweet the sound
  That saved a wretch like me!
I once was lost, but now am found,
  Was blind, but now I see.

The words of John Newton's great hymn about grace are known to millions of people, secular people as well as churchgoers. But theologian and popular author J. I. Packer is certainly right when he notes, in *Knowing God*, that for most of our contemporaries "amazing grace" is no longer amazing. It is "boring grace" instead.

How can that be? How can a theme that has thrilled people for centuries be thought boring? If you talk to church people about next year's operating budget, you will find them interested. You can interest them in social programs or building a new addition to the educational wing. You can talk to them about the latest baseball scores or Wall Street or national politics. But try to discuss the grace of God and you will discover that they are suddenly in a field of discourse quite beyond their capacities. They will not contradict you. They will listen. But they have nothing to contribute. Often you will be met only with blank stares.

What could have caused such indifference, particularly among church-goers? Packer believes it is a failure to understand and "feel in one's heart" four great truths that the meaning of grace presupposes:

1. The sin of man.

Modern people are complacent about their grim spiritual condition. They assume that God is also. The thought that man is a fallen creature in rebellion against God's rightful rule never enters their heads. It did for John Newton, of course, which is why he spoke of himself as "a wretch" who was "lost" and spiritually "blind."

2. The judgment of God.

Most of our contemporaries have lost appreciation for all cause-and-effect links, especially in moral areas. So the idea of a final judgment of God at the end of human history at which sin is punished seems quite fantastic to them.

3. The spiritual inability of man.

Our culture has taught us that for man "all things are possible." We are the masters of our own fate, the captains of our own ship. So the idea that we need the grace of God in order to get right with God, since we cannot save ourselves, seems . . . well, it just seems wrong, frankly. We assume that it will always be possible for us to mend our relationships with God.

4. The sovereign freedom of God.

In this day of multiple human "rights," we also assume that God owes us something, salvation or at least a chance at salvation. But Packer rightly notes that God does not owe us anything. He shows favor to many—that is what this book is about—but he does not need to. The freedom of God to give or withhold favor is the very essence of what grace is about.

Few things, I believe, are more greatly needed in today's nearly moribund church than to recover an appreciation for God's grace, which is why I have written this book.

People who are familiar with my other writings will note that from time to time I have drawn on material developed earlier in my other expository works. I do not apologize for this since, in my opinion, for a study like this one it is a strength rather than a weakness. It means that the material presented here in theological form has emerged from a much larger body of strictly exegetical work and therefore rightly reflects that important and essential biblical foundation.

I have avoided the use of footnotes in this book in order to improve its readability. But from time to time I refer to material that the reader may want to look at firsthand. In chapter 4, I refer to arguments in John Owen's classic study *The Death of Death in the Death of Christ.* It is published by the Banner of Truth Trust (1964) and is volume 10 of the series titled *The Works of John Owen.* Owen's discussion of unbelief is on page 174.

In chapter 5, the story of Ironside and the gypsy is drawn from his book *In the Heavenlies: Practical Expository Addresses on the Epistle to the Ephesians* (Loizeaux Brothers) and can be found on pages 96–98. The story of Henry Moorehouse and the little girl from the slums of London is told by Donald Grey Barnhouse in the booklet, "How God Saves Men" (The Bible Study Hour, 1955), pages 7–9.

The story of Barnhouse's conversion, in chapter 6, is told in volume 5 of his studies of the book of Romans, *God's Grace: Exposition of Bible Doctrines* (Eerdmans, 1959), pages 86–88. His story of the man who was afraid to get married because of his sinful past, in chapter 8, is told in *God's Methods for Holy Living* (Eerdmans, 1951), pages 72–74.

Several of the stories about giving in chapter 14 are from a helpful study of Christian stewardship by Stephen Olford, titled *The Grace of Giving: Biblical Expositions* (Encounter Ministries, 1972). The story of Frances Ridley Havergal is on pages 71–72, the story of General Gordon is on page 51, and the story of the Iron Cross is on page 18.

In chapter 16 the quote from C. S. Lewis, *The Weight of Glory and Other Addresses* (Macmillan/Collier Books, 1980), is on pages 16–17. The entire essay is on pages 3–19.

In the final chapter some of the material regarding the word *Amen* is from volume 10 of Donald Grey Barnhouse's Romans studies, *God's Glory: Exposition of Bible Doctrines* (Eerdmans, 1964), pages 116–121.

These chapters were originally presented as sermons to the congregation of Tenth Presbyterian Church, Philadelphia, in the late winter, spring, and summer of 1992. I want to thank the members and boards of our church for giving me the necessary time to prepare and write these sermons.

"May the grace of the Lord Jesus Christ, and the love of God, and the fellowship of the Holy Spirit" be with us all (2 Cor. 13:14).

James Montgomery Boice
Philadelphia, Pennsylvania

Part One

OUR GRACIOUS GOD

Chapter 1

SURPRISED BY GRACE

---

*The LORD God made garments of skin for Adam and
his wife and clothed them. GENESIS 3:21*

Here is a trivia question you can ask your friends at your
next dinner party. Of all the songs ever written, which song
has been recorded most—by the largest number of different
vocal artists? The answer, as you might expect from the title
of this book, is *Amazing Grace*, the classic Christian hymn
written in 1779 by the former slave trader turned preacher
John Newton.

> Amazing grace! how sweet the sound
> That saved a wretch like me!
> I once was lost but now am found,
> Was blind, but now I see.

Amazing grace really is amazing. It is the most amazing thing in
this vast universe, more amazing even than neutrons and neutrinos,
quarks and quasars, and black holes, each with its own baffling
wonders and surprises. But like all familiar things, grace has lost its

ability to enthrall most people. Instead, as theologian J. I. Packer has said, amazing grace has become "boring grace" for many persons.

If you are one for whom grace has become boring or even someone who has never even thought much about it, I hope this book will be an eye-opener. More than that, I hope it will help you find the amazing, saving grace of God in Jesus Christ. If you have found it already, I hope it will help you come to know and appreciate the grace of God more fully. In these pages I want to look at what God tells us about grace in the Bible and show how grace is what you and I need, more than anything we can possibly imagine—more than a good job, many friends, a nice house, excellent health, self-esteem, someone to love, or whatever.

Grace is present in Jesus Christ for all who will have it because the God of grace is, well, a gracious God.

Grace upon Grace

I am a preacher. So whenever I come to a tremendous word like this, I look in hymnbooks to see what has been written about it by Christians who have gone before me. I was surprised by the many words for grace and the many varieties of grace that were listed.

The *Trinity Hymnal*, used in our church, lists hymns about grace under the headings of *converting grace, the covenant of grace, efficacious grace, the fullness of grace, magnified grace, refreshing grace, regenerating grace, sanctifying grace, saving grace*, and *sovereign grace*. It also has combined listings, such as *the love and grace of God, the love and grace of Christ, the love and grace of the Holy Spirit*, and *salvation by grace*.

A number of descriptive phrases appear in the hymns themselves, such as *abounding grace, abundant grace, amazing grace* (the title of John Newton's hymn), *boundless grace, fountain of grace,*

God of grace, indelible grace, marvelous grace, matchless grace, overflowing grace, pardoning grace, plenteous grace, unfailing grace, unmeasurable grace, wonderful grace, wondrous grace, the word of grace, grace all sufficient, and *grace alone.*

Even Francis Scott Key, the author of the national anthem of the United States, wrote an important hymn about grace:

> Praise the grace whose threats alarmed thee,
> Roused thee from thy fatal ease,
> Praise the grace whose promise warmed thee,
> Praise the grace that whispered peace.

My favorite hymn about grace, as far as the words go, was written by Samuel Davies, a former president of Princeton University.

> Great God of wonders! All thy ways
> Are worthy of thyself—divine:
> And the bright glories of thy grace
> Among thine other wonders shine;
> Who is a pardoning God like thee?
> Or who has grace so rich and free?

Theologians speak of common grace, electing grace, irresistible grace, persevering grace, prevenient grace, pursuing grace, and saving grace. Yet even with these terms, I have not exhausted the Christian terminology.

A Need for Grace

If grace is as important as I have been suggesting, it will not surprise you if I begin where grace first appears, in the early chapters of the book of Genesis.

The first and second chapters of Genesis tell about God's

creation of Adam and Eve, our first parents. They were perfect originally, which we would expect of something made by God, and they were placed in a perfect environment with meaningful work to do. They were what we might call God's regents in creation. They were to rule over the creation, care for the Garden of Eden, and name the animals. We are not to think of this last task in a silly manner, as if they merely pulled names out of the blue and tacked them onto whatever animals came by. Naming something in a meaningful way is not easy. If they were to name the animals, presumably they were to study and classify them according to their true biological relationships.

Adam and Eve had a perfect and beautiful environment in which to work, a loving companion with whom to work, and interesting work to do.

Would that we had it so good!

But there was a catch. Although Adam and Eve were given what seemed to be a maximum amount of freedom to live and act as they pleased, they were nevertheless made by God and were responsible to God for what they did. God gave them something to remind them of this relationship. He placed a tree in the middle of the Garden of Eden with instructions that they were not to eat from it. His warning was, "You are free to eat from any tree in the garden; but you must not eat from the tree of the knowledge of good and evil, for when you eat of it you will surely die" (Gen. 2:16-17).

Well! Not eat of that tree? And without any explanation of why not? The command seemed arbitrary and, no doubt, offensive. At any rate, it must have seemed so to Adam, for there is no suggestion anywhere in the story that he was deceived by the devil's talk, as Eve was. He ate simply because the command had been given, and he was offended by it. Why shouldn't he do what he wanted to do? Especially since it was "his garden" and he was in charge of what went on there!

I understand him. One spring, when I was in the sixth grade, our school principal came into the classroom just before we were to be released to go home for lunch. He had heard that some of the students had been playing with firecrackers, and he wanted to make sure we knew that this was definitely not allowed. Firecrackers were dangerous. They were against Pennsylvania state law. If any of his students brought a firecracker into school, even if he did not set it off, he would be expelled from school immediately.

I did not own any firecrackers. I had not even been thinking about firecrackers. But, you know, once a person starts thinking along that line, firecrackers become an intriguing subject. As I thought about it, I remembered one of my friends who had some.

On the way home from school a friend and I went by this other friend's house, picked up a firecracker, and returned to school with it forty-five minutes after the principal's announcement. We went into the cloakroom, invited a friend to come in with us, and said, "You hold the firecracker by the middle of the fuse. Pinch it very tight. Then we will light it. The others will think that it is going to explode. But when it burns down to your fingers it will go out, and everything will be all right."

What we had not counted on was that the fire would burn our friend's fingers. When we lit the fuse, it did. Our friend dropped the firecracker. It exploded in an immense cloud of blue smoke and tiny bits of white paper, in the midst of which we emerged from the closet, shaken and a bit deaf.

You cannot imagine how loud a firecracker sounds in an old public school building with high ceilings, marble floors, and plaster walls.

Nor can you imagine how quickly a principal can get out of his office, down the hall, and into one of the classrooms. The principal was in our classroom before my friends and I had staggered through the cloakroom's open door. He was as stunned as we were, though for a different reason. I recall him saying over and over, after we had been sent home and had come back to his office with our parents, "I had just made the announcement. I had just told them not to bring any firecrackers into school. I just can't believe it." He couldn't believe it then. But I am sure that our rebellion, as well as other acts of rebellion by children over the years, eventually turned him into a staunch, Bible-believing Calvinist—at least so far as the doctrine of total depravity of children is concerned.

Eve does not seem to have been quite so rebellious. But she sinned, too, because the devil deceived her. We know how he approached her. He began with a question that cast doubt on God's goodness. "Did God really say, 'You must not eat from any tree in the garden'?" (Gen. 3:1). I suppose the emphasis was upon the word *really*, spoken in a somewhat incredulous tone of voice. "Really?" Satan was saying. "I find it hard to believe a command like that. It's so unreasonable. Could God possibly mean that?"

By the time Eve had straightened the devil out, explaining that God had not forbidden them to eat of every tree in the Garden but only that one tree in the middle of the Garden, the damage was already done, and she had begun to wonder if God was really a benevolent God after all.

Satan's next thrust was to cast doubt on God's word. God had said, "You must not eat from the tree of the knowledge of good and evil, for when you eat of it you will surely die." Now Satan said, "You will *not* surely die" (v. 4).

Here was a problem! God had said, "You will die." The devil said, "You will not die." Whom was the woman to believe? We know what she did. Instead of believing and obeying God implicitly, which she should have done, she decided to submit the matter to her own judgment and so examined the tree, finding it to be "good for food and pleasing to the eye, and also desirable for gaining wisdom" (v. 6). That is, she submitted it to a pragmatic test (did it have nutritional value?), an aesthetic test (how would it look on the table?), and an intellectual test (would she learn anything by eating it?). When the fruit of the tree passed those tests, she decided that the devil was right after all and so took some, ate it, and gave it to her husband, who ate also.

And yet, maybe Adam was himself also moved by something Satan said, if Eve reported it to him. Satan had said, "For God knows that when you eat of it your eyes will be opened, and you will be like God, knowing good and evil" (v. 5). Perhaps that is what Adam wanted to be, like God. Never mind that he had been created in the image of God already! As long as he was unable to do exactly what he wanted to, without any limitations whatever, he thought that he was not really like God. And as long as he was not really like God, the only way he could assert himself as God was by resisting the only command God had given and so eating from the forbidden tree.

Over the centuries the devil has undoubtedly gotten a great deal more sophisticated in his temptations. But these initial three temptations worked so well that he repeats them again and again. We hear them constantly.

Temptation number one:

"God is not good. If he were good, he would not tell me not to do something I want to do. I will never be happy unless I get to do it. God must not want me to be happy."

Temptation number two:

"God lies. God may have given us the Bible, but the Bible does not say the same thing as today's psychiatrists, scientists, authors, artists, and politicians. It is contradicted by today's newspapers, books, movies, and television shows. The Bible must be wrong."

9

Temptation number three:

"I cannot be fulfilled unless I am free to do anything I take it into my mind to do, regardless of what it may do to other people. I want what I want when I want it. I want to be God."

As soon as we analyze these temptations and the consequent fall of Adam and Eve into sin, we see that this account in Genesis is not merely a record of something that happened long ago, though it did happen. It is also an accurate description of our condition now. Those temptations are precisely our temptations, and their disobedience and fall is a true picture of the state of all human beings in their rebellion against God.

A Time for Judgment

Whether we like it or not, it is still God's universe. And since God is a just and moral God, it is always the case that sin must be judged. In this case, God came to Adam and Eve at once, demanding to know what they had done. They tried to make excuses, of course, just as we do. God asked Adam where he was, and Adam, who had tried to hide when he heard God coming, explained that he hid because he was naked. God asked, "Who told you that you were naked? Have you eaten from the tree that I commanded you not to eat from?" (v. 11)

Adam could hardly deny the fact. He had eaten from the tree that was in the middle of the Garden. But he pled extenuating circumstances. It was not his fault, he said. He had been misled by the woman. "The woman you put here with me—she gave me some fruit from the tree, and I ate it" (v. 12). Of course, hidden in Adam's excuse was the not-too-subtle implication that in the final analysis the fault must be God's, because he would not have sinned if God had only given him a better woman.

Next God confronted Eve, "What is this you have done?"

Adam had already blamed her, and she could hardly blame him. But Eve could blame the devil, which is what she did. "The serpent deceived me, and I ate" (v. 13). On the surface this seems to have been a better excuse than Adam's. The devil had deceived her. That was better than blaming God. But, of course, it comes to the same thing in the end. For who was responsible for Satan anyway, if not God? Who was it who let him into the Garden?

One of the saddest things about sin is that sinners almost never admit their responsibility for it. Instead, they blame something or someone else.

"I got my bad temper from my father. I can't do anything about it."

"Everyone else is doing it."

"You wouldn't blame me if you saw the neighborhood where I grew up."

Behind all of these excuses is the suggestion that in the final analysis it is God and not ourselves who is responsible for this present evil world. God doesn't take the blame, however. He places it where it belongs. And he judges it, too, as he did in the case of our first parents. In this case he began with the serpent:

> Because you have done this, cursed are you above
> all the livestock and all the wild animals! You will
> crawl on your belly and you will eat dust all the
> days of your life. And I will put enmity between
> you and the woman, and between your offspring
> and hers; he will crush your head, and you will
> strike his heel. (Gen. 3:14-15)

God judged the woman, saying,

> I will greatly increase your pains in childbearing;
> with pain you will give birth to children. Your

desire will be for your husband, and he will rule
over you. (v. 16)

To Adam God said,

Because you listened to your wife and ate from the
tree about which I commanded you, "You must not
eat of it," Cursed is the ground because of you;
through painful toil you will eat of it all the days of
your life. It will produce thorns and thistles for you,
and you will eat the plants of the field. By the sweat
of your brow you will eat your food until you return
to the ground, since from it you were taken; for dust
you are and to dust you will return. (vv. 17-19)

In these three judgments, God decreed suffering for the man
and woman, as well as their offspring, and foretold an eventual
physical death for them and their posterity.

Grace When Least Expected

I suppose that at this point you may be wondering what happened to grace, the theme with which we started, since thus far
the story seems to be one only of sin and tragedy. True, but it is
against the dark background of sin that grace emerges. Grace
means God's favor to the undeserving. So it is only in the context
of sin that grace can be appreciated.

Where is God's grace here? It is in three things.

1. Adam and Eve did not die, at least not immediately.

Some writers have pointed out that Adam and Eve did die
spiritually, which they showed by trying to hide from God when
he came to them in the Garden following their disobedience and
fall. That is true. But physical death was also punishment for sin,

and God had said, "When you eat of it you will surely die." The New King James Version says, "In the day that you eat of it you shall surely die." Adam and Eve must have expected a swift execution of that sentence. Yet after the judgments had been pronounced and God had left them, they were still standing there in the Garden. Fallen, but alive! In other words, they now had time to repent of their sin and believe God about the Savior who would come, just as earlier they had doubted God's word and disobeyed him.

In the next chapter common grace will be discussed. *Common grace* is the grace God shows to all people whether or not they come to personal faith in Jesus Christ as their Savior. But already we have an example of common grace in the way God gave Adam and Eve time to repent and believe him.

It is the same today. If you are not a believer in Christ and are nevertheless alive, that alone is an example of the common grace of God. If you are not in hell, where your sins will eventually take you if you do not repent, it is because God is gracious. One day you will die and be judged, but today is still a day of spiritual opportunity.

2. God promised a Redeemer who would undo the devil's work.

The second great demonstration of the grace of God in the account of Adam and Eve's fall is the promise of a Redeemer found in verse 15. Theologians call this the *protoevangelium*, the first announcement of the gospel in the Bible. At this point Adam and Eve could not have known very much about what God was promising. They did not know when the Redeemer would come. They probably thought their firstborn son was the Redeemer, because they named him Cain, which means "acquired" or "here he is." To their dismay Cain turned out to be the world's first murderer. Adam and Eve did not know the name of the Savior either. That name was not revealed until thousands of years had gone by, when the angel of God told a man named Joseph and a woman named Mary, "You are to give him the name Jesus, because he will save his people from their sins" (Matt. 1:21; cf. Luke 1:31). Still, Adam and Eve knew enough to believe that God would send a Savior and that their only hope of salvation was in him.

That is why Adam named his wife Eve (Gen. 3:20). Eve means "life" or "life giver," and Adam named her Eve because of the promise of God to send a life-giving Savior through her. It was Adam's way of saying that, although he had disbelieved and disobeyed God earlier, he wanted to believe him now. He was willing to stake his spiritual destiny on this first, unembellished promise of a Savior.

3. God saved our first parents.

That is, God justified them on the basis of what Jesus was to do (they looked forward to it), just as God justifies us through faith in what Jesus has done (we look back).

Adam and Eve could not absorb all the details of that atonement, which was yet to come. So God taught them by means of a dramatic illustration. At the end of the story, in verse 21, we are told that after Adam and Eve had believed God, which Adam showed by naming his wife Eve, "The LORD God made garments of skin for Adam and his wife and clothed them." In order to make clothes of skin, God had to kill animals. It was the first death Adam and Eve had witnessed, as far as we know. It must have seemed horrible to them and have made an indelible impression. "So this is what death is; this is what sin causes," they must have exclaimed.

But even more important, the death of the animals must have taught them the principle of substitution, the innocent dying for the guilty, just as the innocent Son of God would one day die for the sins of those God was giving to him. When God clothed our first parents in the animals' skins, Adam and Eve must have had at least a first faint glimmer of the doctrine of imputed righteousness. Later in the Bible we read of our being clothed in Christ's righteousness (cf. Gal. 3:27), and Jesus himself suggested the idea when he referred to the wedding garments worn by those invited to the great marriage supper of the Lamb (cf. Matt. 22:11-12). God saved Adam and Eve from their sins by clothing them in the heavenly righteousness of Jesus Christ, which he symbolized by their being clothed with skins of animals.

Surprising? It must have been mind-boggling to Eve and Adam. The grace of God is always mind-boggling to those who experience it.

Adam and Eve expected to die. Instead they found life.

They must have expected an immediate execution of God's sentence without appeal and without any hope of God's mercy. Instead, they received a promise of a Savior to come and were brought from a state of condemnation to a state of justification by believing in him.

Amazed by Grace

It has always been like this.

Do you remember Thomas? He was the doubting disciple, the one who said that he would not believe in Jesus' resurrection unless he should see the wounds in Christ's hands and be able to thrust his hand into the wound in Christ's side. Why should Thomas have been saved? After all, his cynical words expressed utter disbelief, not faith. Yet even Thomas was surprised by grace when Jesus, instead of condemning him or abandoning him, appeared to him and invited him to perform his empirical test. Instead of doing it, instead of putting his finger or hand in Christ's wounds, Thomas was overwhelmed by grace and fell at Jesus' feet, exclaiming, "My Lord and my God!" (John 20:28).

And how about Peter? Peter had boasted of being able to stand by Jesus even unto death. How little he knew himself! That very night he denied the Lord three times. But although he was rightly ashamed of what he had done and wept bitterly afterwards, Jesus did not cast him off. Instead Jesus came to Peter to recommission him to service.

"Simon son of John, do you love me?" Jesus asked.

"Yes," said Peter.

"Take care of my sheep," said Jesus. Jesus repeated the question and charge three times, corresponding to Peter's three denials (John 21:15-17). Amazing! It was not only grace in salvation that was shown to Peter. It was grace commissioning him to useful service.

And Paul, the first great persecutor of the church? He took his hatred of Christians to the point of securing the condemnation and death of Stephen, the first martyr. And when he had accomplished that, he left for Damascus with the thought of arresting and likewise punishing the believers there. If ever anyone deserved a swift retaliatory judgment, it was Paul. Yet Paul, too, was surprised by grace, as Jesus stopped him on his fiercely bigoted path, calling, "Saul, Saul, why do you persecute me?" (Acts 9:4). And when Paul responded in faith, recognizing that the one he was persecuting was Christ, the very Son of God, Jesus commissioned him to be the first great missionary to the Gentiles. "I will rescue you from your own people and from the Gentiles. I am sending you to them to open their eyes and turn them from darkness to light, and from the power of Satan to God, so that they may receive forgiveness of sins and a place among those who are sanctified by faith in me" (Acts 26:17-18).

Surprised by grace? Yes! That is exactly it. "Surprised by grace" is the story of all who have found salvation through faith in Jesus Christ.

Chapter 2

COMMON GRACE

Though grace is shown to the wicked, they do not learn righteousness; even in a land of uprightness they go on doing evil and regard not the majesty of the LORD.
ISAIAH 26:10

A number of years ago a New York rabbi named Harold S. Kushner made a splash in the publishing world with a book entitled *When Bad Things Happen to Good People*. It was on the *New York Times* best-seller list for months. The thesis of the book was that bad things happen to good people because God is not omnipotent and things simply get away from him. At the end of the book Kushner advises us to forgive God and, like him, just try to get on with life and do the best we can.

How different from what the Bible teaches!

In the thirteenth chapter of Luke there is an incident from the life of Jesus that has no exact parallel anywhere in the New Testament. People had come to Jesus to ask Harold Kushner's question, citing two contemporary examples. In the one example, the soldiers of King Herod had attacked some pilgrims who had come to Jerusalem from Galilee and had killed them when they were in the very act of offering their sacrifices at the temple. In the other example, a tower in the district of Siloam collapsed and killed eighteen apparently innocent passersby.

The fact that the victims seem to have been innocent in both cases was an important part of the question, because the questioners wanted to know why tragedies like that could happen if God is good and if he is in control of things, as we want to believe. Perhaps he is not a good God. Or is it the case—such things are possible—that these apparently good people were actually secret sinners and that this was God's way of striking them down for their transgressions?

For people accustomed to reason as most of us do, Jesus' answer was startling. He replied,

> Do you think that these Galileans were worse sin-
> ners than all the other Galileans because they suf-
> fered this way? . . . Or those eighteen who died
> when the tower in Siloam fell on them—do you
> think they were more guilty than all the others
> living in Jerusalem? I tell you, no! But unless you
> repent, you too will all perish. (Luke 13:2-5)

Jesus was saying that we are actually asking the wrong question when we ask why bad things happen to good people. The question is not why bad things happen to good people but why good things happen to bad people. We are all bad people, and good things happen to us every day of our lives. And in profusion! The real question is: Why didn't the tower fall on us? Why weren't we struck down by Herod's soldiers? Indeed, why did God allow such wicked persons as ourselves to awake this morning, get out of bed, go to work, and add to the mushrooming misery of the world?

The answer is grace, of course. God is a gracious God—gracious even to sinners. But the answer we are seeking goes even further than these statements. In theological language, we are talking about *common grace*, the fact that God "causes his sun to rise on the evil and the good, and sends rain on the righteous and the unrighteous" (Matt. 5:45), and the question we are asking is why common grace is so very common. We are asking God's purpose in allowing so many good things to happen to bad people.

Good Things Do Happen

When I began looking at this subject I was surprised to find that very few books of theology consider common grace. An exception is Louis Berkhof, who discussed it under three headings: (1) the nature of common grace, (2) the means of common grace, and (3) the effects of common grace. But most books of theology skip it, understandably, I suppose. Theologians stress the special grace of God in salvation. Nevertheless, the neglect of common grace is surprising if only because the early Christians seem to have used common grace as a natural starting point for preaching the gospel to Gentiles. Two examples of it are:

1. Paul's sermon at Lystra.

Acts 14 tells of the arrival of Paul and Barnabas at Lystra in Asia Minor on the first missionary journey. Usually Paul began his work in a given city by preaching in the Jewish synagogue, if there was one. But in this case, the missionaries were confronted by a lame man almost as soon as they had entered the city, and Paul healed him. When the crowds saw it, they assumed they had been visited by the gods and called out in their Lycaonian language, "The gods have come down to us in human form!" (Acts 14:11).

In the ancient world almost everyone spoke Greek, even if it wasn't their native tongue. But here in Lycaonia the people seem to have been more at home in their tribal language, for when the miracle took place and they began to babble to themselves about it, at first Paul and Barnabas did not understand what was going on. They noticed that the people were impressed. But when the people said in their own language, "The gods have come down to us in human form" (v. 11), the missionaries did not understand what they were saying.

The apostles were therefore innocently proceeding on their way when they came upon a procession moving out of the city toward them. A priest was leading an animal that had been made ready for sacrifice. The apostles must have thought, *We seem to have come here on a feast day, a religious day. They are practicing their pagan rites. We will have to speak to them about that in time.* But they soon discovered to their horror that the people were coming to do sacrifice to them.

Why to them? Because they believed, as the missionaries quickly discovered, that Barnabas was Zeus in human form. Zeus was the greatest of the gods. And Paul, who was the chief speaker, was presumed to be Hermes (Mercury), the gods' spokesman.

This could have happened in any ancient city, but it is particularly significant that it happened here because of something the Roman poet Ovid wrote in his celebrated masterpiece *Metamorphoses* (viii, 620–724). In this work Ovid collected the mythological stories that had to do with people being changed into something else, and at one place he records a story concerning this very area. According to Ovid's story, Zeus and Hermes had visited a valley near Lystra. They went from door to door, but the people refused to take them in. Finally, they came to a very poor house occupied by a man named Philemon and his wife, Baucis. These elderly people received the two gods, and they stayed the night. In the morning the gods took the couple out of the city to a mountain, and when they looked back on the valley, they saw that Zeus and Hermes had flooded it, drowning every-one. Then, while they were still looking on, Philemon and Baucis saw that the gods had transformed their poor hovel into a great temple with a glittering gold roof.

This story must have been known in Lystra. So when Paul and Barnabas healed the lame man, the people inevitably thought that Zeus and Hermes had returned. And if they had, the last thing in the world they wanted to do was offend them, because they remembered what had happened the first time around.

When the missionaries discovered what was going on, they were aghast. They tore their clothes and rushed out into the crowd, shouting: "Men, why are you doing this? We too are only men, human like you" (v. 15).

Then Paul began to preach.

This sermon should be compared with the sermon in chapter 13, spoken to a largely Jewish audience. In that chapter Paul quotes the Old Testament frequently, rehearsing God's great acts in the Old Testament period. That is not the case here. Here Paul is speaking to a Gentile or pagan audience that had no knowledge of the Scriptures. He could not have told these people about God's acts in Old Testament times because they would not have known what he was talking about. So he started where they did have understanding and spoke of God as the Creator of all things and as the source of common grace:

> We are bringing you good news, telling you to
> turn from these worthless things to the living God,
> who made heaven and earth and sea and everything
> in them. In the past, he let all nations go their own
> way. Yet he has not left himself without testimony:
> He has shown kindness by giving you rain from
> heaven and crops in their seasons; he provides you
> with plenty of food and fills your hearts with joy.
> (Acts 14:15-17)

This is a substantial statement of what common grace is about. It has at least these four elements.

Rain from heaven. It is hard to imagine that Paul said this without knowing and perhaps consciously remembering Jesus' words about God causing "his sun to rise on the evil and the good" and sending "rain on the righteous and the unrighteous" (Matt. 5:45). Clearly God does not discriminate between people in the distribution of nature's blessings.

Crops in their seasons. The ancients attributed the regular rotation of the seasons to their nature gods, sometimes to nature itself. But Paul says that the seasons and the annual summer or fall harvests flow from God's grace to all persons. Even the wicked are able to sow and harvest their crops in the right seasons and profit by them.

Joy. This may refer to the joy of harvesttime specifically, but it probably has a broader meaning. We remember James saying that "every good and perfect gift is from above, coming down from the Father of the heavenly lights, who does not change like shifting shadows" (James 1:17). This means that every joy, every pleasure, every happiness in life is from God, whether we know or acknowledge it or not. These three things—rain from heaven, the crops in their seasons, and joy—testify both to God's existence and to the essential goodness of his nature.

Delay of judgment. The fourth expression of common grace is the delay of God's judgment, which Paul expressed by saying that "in the past, he [God] let all nations go their own way." It brings us back to Jesus' teaching about the Galileans who were killed by Herod's soldiers. The amazing thing is not that bad things happened to these people, but that so many good things happen to everyone. And the most amazing thing of all is that God had tolerated the evil of the unbelieving, Gentile world for so long and had postponed (and continues to postpone) judging it severely.

2. Paul's sermon in Athens.

A few chapters further on, in Acts 17, we have an account of Paul's sermon on Mars Hill in Athens. It also deals with common grace, following a line similar to Paul's sermon at Lystra.

After calling the people's attention to their altar "TO AN UNKNOWN GOD" and declaring his intention of proclaiming this "unknown God" to them, Paul said:

> The God who made the world and everything in it
> . . . is not served by human hands, as if he needed
> anything, because he himself gives all men life and
> breath and everything else. From one man he
> made every nation of men, that they should inhabit
> the whole earth; and he determined the times set
> for them and the exact places where they should
> live. (Acts 17:24-26)

This sermon does not mention rainfall and the seasons, probably because the life of Athens was far less agricultural than life at Lystra. But the theme is similar. In this sermon Paul mentions:

The breath of life. We may use our breath to curse God, but even the atheist who shakes his fist at heaven, shouting, "There is no God," does so with the breath, speech, intellect, and strength that God has given him.

A place to live. This is a significant statement about the territories possessed by the world's nations. These are not arbitrary possessions, still less the rightful spoils of war, according to Paul's teaching. Rather they are the gift of a gracious God to all the world's peoples. The bottom line is that we should be thankful to God for such bounty.

Everything else. Paul may have elaborated this in the actual delivery of his sermon, since the biblical accounts are undoubtedly shortened versions of what happened. But we can supply what this includes ourselves, since it is similar to James' mention of "every good and perfect gift" (James 1:17).

What in your life do you regard as very good? Make a list.

Your job? It has been given you by God. If you reply that you got it by hard work and by possessing talents and skills that someone else did not have, I reply that it is God who has given you those skills and endowed you with both the will and capacity to work hard.

Your family? The people you love were created by God and have been given to you as a part of his benevolent ordering of life's events.

Times to relax and enjoy the results of your hard labors? It is God who has made relaxation possible by prospering the culture in which you live and by giving you enough free time to enjoy your possessions.

Peace? God is the author of peace.

Whatever good thing you can think of, it is God who has given it to you or made it possible for you to enjoy it. You enjoy it only because God is a gracious God. If he were some other kind of god, your very existence would be unimaginably different.

There is one more thing we need to learn about common grace from Paul's sermon on Mars Hill. It is in the words that immediately follow those I quoted earlier. Having spoken of grace, Paul concluded, "God did this so that men would seek him and perhaps reach out for him and find him, though he is not far from each one of us. For in him we live and move and have our being" (Acts 17:27-28). This is important. For it is a way of saying that God also has a good purpose in his good actions. He wants us to recognize his goodness, to turn from sin, to reach out and find him, and so be able to express our gratitude in true faith and proper obedience.

Paul writes the same thing in Romans, observing that the "kindness, tolerance and patience" of God are meant to lead us to repentance (Rom. 2:4).

Even Bad Things Can Be Good Things

We do not repent, of course. But before we explore that sad fact, there is something else that needs to be noted about common grace. Up to now we have been considering the truth that good things happen even to bad people. But bad things also happen to them, to remind us of the destructive nature of sin, the shortness of life, and the need for redemption, so that we will seek God and find him, if not through the unmixed good things, then through the bad things.

Earlier I suggested some of the things God's common grace supplies: a job, your family, times to enjoy life's pleasures, and personal peace. Clearly, each of these can also be taken away. But if they were, losing them should have a good rather than a bad effect on those who do not know God.

The loss of a job should teach us of the uncertainty of everything in life and of the need to seek our only true or lasting security in God. The loss of a family member should remind you of eternity and of the need to prepare for it. That is why we often read words from Psalm 90 at funeral services:

> The length of our days is seventy years—
> or eighty, if we have the strength;
> yet their span is but trouble and sorrow,
> for they quickly pass, and we fly away. . . .
> Teach us to number our days aright,
> that we may gain a heart of wisdom. (Ps. 90:10, 12)

The loss of good things should turn you from the rampant materialism that surrounds you and remind you that "a man's life does not consist in the abundance of his possessions," as Jesus said (Luke 12:15).

The loss of peace, whether personal or political, should cause you to seek "peace with God" through the work of Jesus Christ

(Rom. 5:1) and to pray for the "peace of God, which transcends all understanding" (Phil. 4:7).

Toward the end of the Old Testament there is a minor prophet who deals with these subjects just as I have been treating them in this chapter. It is Joel. The land had experienced a devastating invasion of locusts in Joel's day, probably identical to a notable invasion of Palestine by locusts in 1915, as described by John D. Whiting in the December 1915 issue of *National Geographic* magazine. In 1915, the locusts consumed everything in the region so that there was literally nothing to eat. In a predominantly agricultural economy, which Judah's was, this was an unmitigated disaster, and Joel does not hesitate to call it exactly that. In fact, in his opening chapter he calls on various classes in the society to recognize the evil as evil and weep because of it.

But that is not all he wants. As the prophecy continues, Joel makes three more important points: (1) God is responsible for the disaster. (2) Although it was dreadful, the invasion of the locusts would be followed in time by an even greater disaster: God's final judgment. He calls it "the day of the LORD" and describes it as "a day of darkness and gloom, a day of clouds and blackness" (Joel 2:1-2). (3) The present evil and the greater coming evil should lead people to repent of their sin and seek God. Joel's classic words are:

> Rend your heart and not your garments. Return to the LORD your God, for he is gracious and compassionate, slow to anger and abounding in love, and he relents from sending calamity. Who knows? He may turn and have pity and leave behind a blessing. (Joel 2:13-14)

The people did not return, of course. They continued in their perverse, unrepentant ways, and the result was the destruction of Jerusalem and the deportation of the nation as a result of the Babylonian invasion of 586 B.C.

Bad People Misuse Good Things

This brings us to the final text I want to consider in this study of common grace:

> Though grace is shown to the wicked, they do not learn righteousness; even in a land of uprightness they go on doing evil and regard not the majesty of the Lord. (Isa. 26:10)

Jesus once compared his ministry and that of John the Baptist. John was an austere figure who lived in the desert and preached a sober message of repentance from sin. Jesus moved among the masses and participated in such joyful affairs as weddings. But the people did not listen to either John or Jesus. So Jesus said:

> To what can I compare this generation? They are like children sitting in the marketplaces and calling out to others: "We played the flute for you, and you did not dance; we sang a dirge, and you did not mourn." For John came neither eating nor drinking, and they say, "He has a demon." The Son of Man came eating and drinking, and they say, "Here is a glutton and a drunkard, a friend of tax collectors and 'sinners.'" (Matt. 11:16-19)

It is the exact point I have been making. People do not respond to common grace. It does not matter whether common grace expresses itself in the good things of life that should lead us to seek out and thank God who is the source of all good things, or whether it expresses itself in bad things, like natural disasters, that are intended as a warning of the even greater disaster of God's final judgment. The wicked respond to neither, as Isaiah says. Therefore, if anyone is going to be saved from sin and brought to true faith in God and obedience, it is going to be by *special grace* and not by *common grace*, that is, by the electing grace of God, which reaches down to regenerate lost sinners and turn them from their destructive ways.

I return to the situation at Lystra.

After Paul and Barnabas had stopped the crowd from sacrificing to them as if they were gods, they taught them the Word of God. But enemies of the gospel from Antioch and Iconium came to Lystra and turned the crowd against the two missionaries. As a result, the same crowd, which days before was ready to worship Barnabas as Zeus and Paul as Hermes, then stoned Paul and dragged him outside the city and left him for dead. What fickle people these were! Yet they were no different from people in our time. People are always fickle until God brings true stability into their lives through the gospel. If anything of any permanence is to happen—if lives are to be changed, if the seed of the Word is to fall into good soil and bear fruit, and do it year after year—it will only be through the special electing and regenerating grace of God.

This is what happened in Lystra, as well as in the other cities Paul was visiting. Because of the stoning, Paul left Lystra the next day. He went to Derbe and taught there. But shortly thereafter, we read that Paul and Barnabas went back through the cities they had visited, including Lystra, "strengthening the disciples and encouraging them to remain true to the faith" (Acts 14:22). This means that God had worked in the lives of some of these unstable, pagan people to bring them to faith in Jesus Christ.

Common grace saves no one. But although common grace saves no one, the special grace of God operating by the preaching and teaching of the Word of God does, which is why we must study it carefully in the next chapters.

Chapter 3

THE DAWN OF GRACE

The law was given through Moses; grace and truth came through Jesus Christ. JOHN 1:17

Dispensationalists tend to emphasize the differences between the Old Testament and the New Testament, and there is a corresponding tendency among reformed thinkers to minimize or deny them. But in one area even the most rigorous reformed theologians must acknowledge a difference between the Testaments, and that is in the emphasis on law in the Old Testament and the emphasis on grace in the New.

The reason?

It is the teaching of the New Testament itself. John made the distinction when he wrote, "The law was given through Moses; grace and truth came through Jesus Christ" (John 1:17).

Since I am a reformed theologian myself, I do not want to overemphasize this distinction. I know that the Old Testament is also profoundly aware of grace. Even more important, it teaches that the way of salvation is by the grace of God in providing an atoning Savior, who turns out to be Jesus. We saw this in our opening study of Genesis 3, and it could be proved throughout the Old Testament by many other passages. And by the New Testament! In Romans Paul teaches that Abraham, David, and the other Old Testament saints were saved exactly as God saves people today, that is, through believing on Jesus Christ (Rom. 4:1-8). They looked forward to his coming. We look back. But the basis of our salvation and the nature of belief are the same.

I am also aware that the New Testament does not reject the law of God or deny its importance. In Romans, the same book in which Paul teaches that salvation is by grace and that the Old Testament figures were saved by faith, as we are, the apostle asks, "Do we, then, nullify the law by this faith?" and answers, "Not at all! Rather, we uphold the law" (Rom. 3:31). Later he writes, "So then, the law is holy, and the commandment is holy, righteous and good" (Rom. 7:12). We must never overstate the difference.

Yet we must not overlook it either. For there clearly is a difference, as our text indicates.

Some Lexical Data

The contrast between the Old Testament emphasis on law and the New Testament emphasis on grace can be seen at least in part by the frequency with which the word *grace* is used in each Testament.

In the New International Version there are only eight occurrences of the word *grace* in the Old Testament, none terribly significant. But there are 128 uses of *grace* in the NIV's New Testament translation. Moreover, they occur in key passages and with multiple usage. Romans 5 is one example. The word is used seven times in that chapter. *Grace* is also used extensively in Ephesians 2. It occurs four times in the Greek text of John 1.

Most striking of all are the doxologies. There are thirty that use the word *grace*, doxologies such as: "Grace and peace to you from God our Father and from the Lord Jesus Christ" (Rom. 1:7); "The grace of our Lord Jesus be with you" (Rom. 16:20); "May the grace of the Lord Jesus Christ, and the love of God, and the fellowship of the Holy Spirit be with you all" (2 Cor. 13:14); "The grace of the Lord Jesus Christ be with your spirit. Amen" (Phil. 4:23); "Grace, mercy and peace from God the Father and Christ Jesus our Lord" (1 Tim. 1:2); and "Grace be with you" (2 Tim. 4:22).

There are other Old Testament words for grace, of course.

The word *gracious* is found thirty-nine times in the Old Testament (NIV), seven times as an exact or near repetition of Exodus 34:6 ("The LORD, the LORD, the compassionate and gracious God, slow to anger, abounding in love and faithfulness, maintaining love to thousands, and forgiving wickedness, rebellion and sin"). Those words are repeated more or less in Nehemiah 9:17, Psalms 86:15, 103:8, and 145:8, Joel 2:13, and Jonah 4:2. But even these texts do not add up to the force grace seems to have when it breaks forth freshly with the coming of Jesus Christ.

In the same way, *favor* is used ninety-eight times in the Old Testament. But many of these are of human favor only, and the double use of the word has the effect of weakening it even when it is applied to God.

So there really is a difference between the Old Testament and the New Testament at this point, and John is not overstating the matter when he writes of grace coming in a special way with Jesus Christ.

> We have seen his glory, the glory of the One and
> Only, who came from the Father, full of grace and
> truth. . . . From the fullness of his grace we have all
> received one blessing after another. For the law

> was given through Moses; grace and truth came
> through Jesus Christ. (John 1:14, 16-17)

John meant that grace came to us fully with Jesus Christ, because it is through his death and by his resurrection that sinful men and women have been made righteous before God.

Peter's Revealing Speech

In the fifteenth chapter of Acts there is a revealing statement of how this change must have struck the early Christians. The Council of Jerusalem was in session, and it had been debating whether the ceremonial requirements of the Old Testament should be imposed on Gentile Christians. Paul and his fellow missionaries had been preaching the gospel to Gentiles, Gentiles had been turning to Christ, and churches that were largely Gentile were being established. Paul had not been requiring these Gentile Christians to come under the legal Jewish obligations such as circumcision, keeping the Sabbath, observing Jewish feast days, and kosher cooking. His opponents, known as the legalistic party, were insisting that these were essential, arguing that no one could be saved without observing them.

At last the council decided in favor of Gentile liberty, but not until after Peter had told how God led him to preach to Gentiles in the home of Cornelius and how God had saved Cornelius and his family apart from circumcision or ceremonial purifications (Acts 10). Peter said,

> Now then, why do you try to test God by putting
> on the necks of the disciples a yoke that neither we
> nor our fathers have been able to bear? No! We be-
> lieve it is through the grace of our Lord Jesus that
> we are saved, just as they are. (Acts 15:10-11)

The revealing statement is Peter's confession that "neither we nor our fathers have been able to bear" the law's yoke.

We need to remember that Peter and the other Jews who had gathered for this council were pious people. They were not like the heathen or even the uninstructed and indifferent people of Palestine, who were ignorant of the law and did not care that they were. Peter and his fellow believers knew the law and had been trying to keep it. But here Peter led these pious Jews in a confession that they could not keep it. It may be, as Paul told the Romans, that "the law is holy, and the commandment is holy, righteous and good" (Rom. 7:12). But Peter argued that the law did not seem to have been good. It had been a burden instead, and a heavy one at that. Pious Jews had tried to live by the law, but they had failed to do it. That is why the coming of grace by Jesus Christ was so significant to them. It was a lifting of their burden and a doing away with their profound sense of failure.

Jesus Was Himself Gracious

But let's start with Jesus himself, for that is what John seems to do in the wonderful prologue to his Gospel. The opening verses tell of Jesus' deity and preexistence, followed by the appearance of John the Baptist as his forerunner. Then, in John 1:14, John announces the Incarnation, and at once grace is prominent: "The Word became flesh and made his dwelling among us. We have seen his glory, the glory of the One and Only, who came from the Father, full of grace and truth." It would seem from that statement that, according to John, the glory of Jesus was seen first in his own personal graciousness.

We live in a very boorish world, of course. So it is easy to think of people who are not gracious. You have probably had contact with some this past week.

Sales people who have ignored you in the store even when you wanted to buy something or had a question about it.

Drivers who blew their horns at you or even cursed you when you slowed down to find a right turn or to locate an obscure street address.

Business associates who have lied about you to get ahead themselves. There are many people like that. In fact, all of us are like that at least some of the time.

But if you think carefully, you can probably also think of people who have been gracious to you. Perhaps a friend, a marriage partner, or your parents were gracious people. Instead of treating you as you deserved, these people have treated you as you want to be treated. They have overlooked your failures and have instead been kind and helpful.

Well, Jesus was like that. In fact, he was like all these gracious people rolled into one, and then he surpassed even that. He was never cross, never selfish, never impatient with people who had problems, never superior or judgmental. He never told people, "It serves you right" or, "I hope you get what's coming to you" or, "That's your problem" or, "Don't bother me about it." He never disassociated himself from anyone, as if some types or classes of people were below him. Indeed, he moved easily among both the high and the low, and he was so much at home with the lower classes that his enemies used it to attack him, saying that he was a "drunkard" and a "friend of sinners." People liked Jesus. They found him gracious.

Do you want a good description of Jesus? Here it is:

> Love is patient, love is kind. It does not envy, it
> does not boast, it is not proud. It is not rude, it is
> not self-seeking, it is not easily angered, it keeps no
> record of wrongs. Love does not delight in evil but
> rejoices with the truth. It always protects, always

trusts, always hopes, always perseveres. Love never
fails. (1 Cor. 13:4-8)

Another way of saying this is to say that all the fruit of the
Spirit was in Jesus, and the fruit of the Spirit, as Paul tells us, is
"love, joy, peace, patience, kindness, goodness, faithfulness, gen-
tleness and self-control" (Gal. 5:22-23).

Jesus was the perfection of these virtues.

But there is more to the meaning of Jesus' personal graciousness than this. For when John introduces Jesus as "full of grace
and truth," he does so in a verse that is speaking of the Incarnation, that is, in a verse that tells how Jesus is God come down to
us in human form. The importance of that is that it means that
God is gracious, too, for God is like Jesus.

What would we think of God if we had only the law to go on?
We would think of God as a rather demanding, harsh, unbending, and judging deity, which is what most of the Old Testament
figures did think. And we would not be entirely wrong. For the
law *is* demanding. It *is* unbending. That is the very nature of law.
Moreover, the law of God is a law with penalties. The law says,
"Do this and you will live" (Luke 10:28). But if we do not do it,
the law says, "The soul who sins . . . will die" (Ezek. 18:4), and
"The wages of sin is death" (Rom. 6:23).

We cannot fault God for his righteousness or justice. But if
law is all we have to go on, we might be at least partially excused
if we should think of God as rather insensitive to us or unsympa-
thetic to our failures.

But now Jesus has come, and we see in a dramatic way that
the giving of the law is not all there is to say about God. True,
God is a lawgiver, and he did give the law through Moses, and
the law of the Old Testament is "holy, righteous and good." But
God is also gracious, as gracious as Jesus Christ. God is not harsh
or unforgiving, as we suppose. Moreover, his purpose in sending
Jesus was to teach us that he is indeed gracious and to provide a

way for us to be saved from the punishments required by the law, since we cannot either obey the law or save ourselves from condemnation.

Jesus Acted Graciously

When we say that Jesus was himself gracious, we are talking about Jesus' character. But this inner character of Jesus was also expressed outwardly in the way he dealt with people. Therefore, we have to add to the statement that Jesus was personally gracious the additional statement that Jesus acted graciously to others.

One great example occurs only in John's Gospel. Jesus' enemies had been trying to trap him. On one occasion they had sent their temple guards to arrest him. They had been unsuccessful. But here they had finally hit upon a scheme that was literally fiendish. They had managed to catch a young woman in the very act of adultery, and they brought her to Jesus, saying, "Teacher, this woman was caught in the act of adultery. In the Law Moses commanded us to stone such women. Now what do you say?" (John 8:4-5)

This was despicable. Besides, it was probably dishonest. According to the practice of law in Jesus' day, it was not possible to secure a conviction in capital cases unless there were multiple witnesses to the very act for which the person was accused. In this case, there would have had to have been two or more witnesses, and they would have had to have seen not merely what we would call a compromising situation, even so compromising a situation as the couple lying together on the same bed, but also to have seen the couple engaged in physical movements that could have no other possible explanation. How could that have been achieved unless the whole case was a setup? To have achieved that kind of evidence the woman's accusers would have had to have stationed their witnesses in the room or at the keyhole beforehand and thus have trapped the woman.

These difficult legal demands were intentional, of course. For the aim of the lawyers was to make executions virtually impossible. It is how the people managed to exist under the unyielding standards and harsh penalties of God's law. One important Jewish document, the Mishnah, declares, "The Sanhedrin, which so often as once in seven years, condemns a man to death, is a slaughter house" (*Makhoth*, 1, 10).

Besides, where was the man in the relationship? If the witnesses had seen the very act of adultery, as the accusers claimed, they would have had to have seen the man, too. Yet he was not present. Was he in on the plot? The more we think about this attempt to trap Jesus, the more hypocritical, cruel, evil, and demonic it becomes.

But it was shrewd, too! It was shrewd because it was addressing the one truly great problem in the relationship of any sinful human being to God.

The earlier attempts to trap Jesus had not been like this. Earlier his enemies had tried to catch him on the matter of paying taxes. Should a loyal Jew pay taxes to Caesar's government or not? But that involved only the matter of public hostility to Rome, and Jesus handled it easily. He told them to give Caesar his due but to be sure they gave God his due also (Matt. 22:21). After this the Sadducees had tried to catch Jesus with a sophomoric question about the Resurrection, asking who a woman would be married to in heaven if she had been married to more than one husband here. Jesus handled that by his superior knowledge of the Scriptures, telling the Sadducees that they knew neither the Scriptures nor the power of God (Matt. 22:29).

This problem was not like those earlier problems, however. In this test three important matters were at stake: (1) the life of the woman, which was precious, at least to Jesus; (2) Jesus' teaching about the gracious nature of his kingdom; and (3) the law of Moses, which had been given by God.

The way the question was posed, it seemed to the rulers that Jesus would have to sacrifice at least one and possibly two of these three elements. Jesus was known for being gracious. He taught that God was love, and he seemed himself to love sinners. But if Jesus should show love to the woman who had been caught in adultery and recommend that her life be spared, he would be setting himself against the divinely given law of Moses. How could a teacher do that and still pretend to be a prophet sent by God? No one could both oppose the law of God and also speak for God at the same time. Jesus would be identified as a false teacher.

On the other hand, if Jesus should uphold the law, then he would have to sacrifice both the life of the woman and his teaching about the compassionate nature of his kingdom. "Sure, he tells you that God is love and that we should love one another," his enemies would scoff. "But what does he do when the chips are down? He turns on you and says you should be killed. Who needs that? Just look what he did to that poor woman."

That was a real problem, you see. For with demonic insight—this is why I used the words *fiendish* and *demonic* earlier—these men had hit upon the *real* problem, *the* problem of *all* problems in the relationship of a sinful man or woman to God. The problem is: How can God show love to the sinner without being unjust? How can he uphold his law, which is "good," but at the same time also be gracious? Or, as Paul states the problem in Romans 3:26, how can God be both "just and the one who justifies" the ungodly? From a human point of view, the problem is unsolvable. In this the rulers were right. "Jesus cannot show love even if he wants to," they reasoned. But what these rulers would not acknowledge is that in Jesus' case they were not dealing with a mere man, for whom this would have been unsolvable. Rather, they were dealing with God, and "with God all things are possible" (Matt. 19:26).

We know what Jesus did. Instead of replying to the woman's accusers directly, he bent down and wrote on the ground.

I must admit that I do not know what he wrote because the story does not tell us. Some commentators suggest that he wrote on the ground to gain time, though why the eternal Son of God should need time to think through the issues of the case I cannot fathom. Other writers suggest that Jesus wrote out the men's accusations to impress them with the gravity of what they were doing. But they knew how serious their accusations were already; that is why they were making them. Perhaps Jesus wrote out the men's sins, since he knew their hearts and knew acts of which they themselves were guilty.

This is probably the right explanation, because something got through to them eventually. According to the story, they soon began to fade away one at a time, beginning with the oldest. Yet even this is not entirely clear because, strictly speaking, the story tells us that they began to leave, not while Jesus was writing, but later, when he told them, "If any one of you is without sin, let him be the first to throw a stone at her" (John 8:7).

Whatever Jesus wrote and for whatever reason, the woman's accusers eventually did go away, and at the end Jesus was left alone with the woman. He could have accused her, because he was without sin. But instead, he was gracious; indeed, he was "full of grace and truth."

At first he asked her a question. "Woman, where are they? Has no one condemned you?"

"No one," she answered.

Jesus replied, "Then neither do I condemn you. Go now and leave your life of sin" (vv. 10–11).

Jesus' Death Made Grace Possible

It is hard to imagine a more gracious ending to a story. But we have not reached the meat of the story even yet. Jesus was gracious, to be sure. But the question remains: How *could* he be gracious and at the same time do the right thing? He was the very Son of God. How could he defend the woman and yet uphold the law?

Some writers have explained what Jesus did by a legal technicality. The law required two or more witnesses, and since the accusers left the scene under Jesus' scorching gaze and question, in the end there was no one left to accuse her. Jesus could have done it himself. He was sinless, and because he knew the hearts of people, he certainly knew the full circumstances of the woman's guilt, though he had not himself physically witnessed her sin. But Jesus was only one witness even so. Writers who approach the story this way suggest that the legal requirements of the law in regard to witnesses in capital cases freed Jesus from the need to condemn the woman and so permitted him to be gracious. But to reason this way is to miss the true heart of the story, in my judgment.

The question is: Why did Jesus *not* condemn the woman? Why did *he* not cast the first stone? We can understand that he wanted to be gracious. We would want to be ourselves. But how could he forgive her and still uphold the law? As soon as we reflect on that, we realize that the reason he did not condemn the woman is surely the same reason he does not condemn us, if we are among those who have believed on him. Why does Jesus not pronounce a sentence of eternal death on those who come to him in faith today? It is because of his atoning work on the cross by which he was, at that time, soon to take upon himself the punishment for the sins of all whom the Father would give to him. Jesus forgave the woman. But he did not do it easily or in disregard of God's law. He did it because his death was to make forgiveness possible.

This is the gospel, of course. And it is the only solution to how God can remain just and also save the sinner. To us salvation is free. It is by grace. But it is by grace only because the Son of God took the punishment for sin by dying in our place.

Here are some characteristics of the reign of law versus the reign of grace, which came by Jesus Christ.

1. Under law God demands righteousness from his people; under grace God gives righteousness to them.

2. Under law righteousness is based upon Moses and good works; under grace righteousness is based upon Christ and Christ's character.

3. Under law blessings accompany obedience; under grace God bestows blessings as a free gift.

4. Under law there is nothing in men or women by which we can achieve what God demands; under grace that power is made available.

"Leave Your Life of Sin"

We must never think that grace, wonderful as it is, either permits or encourages us to go on sinning. For it is not only "grace" that came through Jesus Christ. "Truth" did also (John 1:17). And the truth in this matter is that God still requires holiness of his people. "Shall we go on sinning so that grace may increase?" asked Paul. He answered, "By no means! We died to sin; how can we live in it any longer?" (Rom. 6:1-2).

This is why the ending of the story of Jesus and the woman trapped in adultery is so important, though it is often overlooked. Jesus did not only forgive her on the basis of his coming death for sin. True, he did forgive her. But having done that, he added, "Go now and leave your life of sin." This always follows upon forgiveness. For God is unchanging, and he continues to be righteous and demand righteousness even when he is forgiving. No one can be saved and then continue to do as he or she pleases. If we are saved, we must stop sinning.

At the same time, we can be grateful that Jesus spoke as he did. For we notice that he did not say, "Leave your life of sin, and I will not condemn you." If he had said that, what hope for us could there be? Our problem is precisely that we do sin. There could be no forgiveness if forgiveness was based upon our ceasing to sin. Instead of that, Jesus actually spoke in the reverse order. First, he granted forgiveness freely, without any conceivable link to our performance. Forgiveness is granted only on the merit of his atoning death. But then, having forgiven us freely, Jesus tells us with equal force to stop sinning.

And here is the greatest wonder. There is nothing that can so motivate us to leave a life of sin as God's forgiveness.

Did the woman do it? I am sure she did. She had experienced grace in Jesus Christ, and that has always proved to be the most transforming life experience in the universe.

Have you learned that "grace and truth" came with Jesus Christ? Not all people have. I suppose it is fair to say that you are at some point in this story, whether you are aware of it or not. You may be in the position of the rulers, not necessarily in using your knowledge of what is right and wrong to come down hard on other people, though you may, but in merely going away when you are confronted by your need for forgiveness. The men in the story needed forgiveness as much as the woman. That is the meaning of their guilty withdrawal. But they did not find it since they left instead.

Or you may be like the crowd. The people were watching. They were spectators. They saw the rulers' conviction and Jesus' compassion. They may even have marveled at both. But they did not enter into the action. Like many today, they stood at a distance and did not get involved.

Fortunately, there was also the woman. You may be like her. I hope you are. Of all the people who were present that day by far the best one to have been was the woman. For she not only witnessed the events. She experienced them, and that meant that she entered into the reality of Jesus' great grace.

The crowd did nothing except go home and forget what it had witnessed.

The rulers went from Jesus into increasing spiritual darkness, and six months later they were back again even more hardened than before to demand the death of the sinless Son of God. They had their law, but it did not save them. It hardened them, and they perished by it.

Only the sinful woman was saved, and it was because she had discovered that, although law had come through Moses and condemned her, grace and truth truly had come through Jesus Christ.

Part Two

SAVING GRACE

Chapter 4

SOVEREIGN GRACE

> *Praise be to the God and Father of our Lord Jesus*
> *Christ, who has blessed us in the heavenly realms with*
> *every spiritual blessing in Christ. For he chose us in him*
> *before the creation of the world to be holy and blameless*
> *in his sight. In love he predestined us to be adopted as his*
> *sons through Jesus Christ, in accordance with his plea-*
> *sure and will—to the praise of his glorious grace, which*
> *he has freely given us in the One he loves. In him we*
> *have redemption through his blood, the forgiveness of*
> *sins, in accordance with the riches of God's grace that he*
> *lavished on us with all wisdom and understanding.*
> *EPHESIANS 1:3-8*

In 1974, six years after I became pastor of Tenth Presbyterian Church, a number of seminarians, pastors, and I launched a conference to promote Calvinistic doctrines, which we felt were being widely neglected by most Christians. We did not know what to call our conference, but since it began in Philadelphia, we decided to call it the Philadelphia Conference on Reformed

Theology. It became quite popular, and in the years since it has been held in such widely scattered cities as San Francisco, Los Angeles, St. Louis, Chicago, Toronto, Memphis, Pittsburgh, and Atlanta, as well as its home city of Philadelphia. At the beginning, we thought our conference must be unique, that there was nothing like it anywhere else.

I have learned since that there have been other such conferences, a number of them sponsored by Calvinistic Baptist churches. I have spoken at some of them. Characteristically, these Baptist gatherings are called "Sovereign Grace" conferences.

The words *sovereign grace*, which is the theme of this chapter, are almost redundant, though necessary. *Sovereign* means "according to the will of the sovereign [that is, God]." It means according to his will and nothing else. *Grace* means "unmerited favor." But think what happens as soon as you begin to tinker with those terms. If you take "sovereign" away from grace so that grace is no longer dependent upon the pure will of God, then grace becomes dependent upon something else, either merit in the subject receiving it or circumstances, and in that case, grace ceases to be grace. It becomes something deserved or necessary. In order to have true grace, grace must be sovereign.

Yet, as I said, both words are necessary simply because we do not often think of spiritual things clearly, and it is natural for us to imagine that the cause of grace is something found in human beings, or that God is somehow obliged to be gracious.

Grace in Ephesians

Sovereign grace is strongly emphasized in Paul's great letter to the Ephesians. In the last chapter I pointed out that *grace* occurs 128 times in the New Testament (NIV) as opposed to only eight occurrences in the Old Testament. But the use of the word is not equally spread throughout the New Testament. In some books the word does not occur at all, Matthew and Mark, for instance. In Luke it is found only once. Sometimes *grace* appears in a doxology or benediction, where it is not explained. At other times it occurs repeatedly in a single passage.

Ephesians is a book in which grace has great importance. In Ephesians, the word occurs eleven times, three times in chapter 1 and three times in chapter 2. These chapters contain very important teaching.

Like Romans, Ephesians deals with the most basic Christian doctrines. I call it "a minicourse in theology, centered on the church." But even more than Romans, Ephesians stresses the sovereignty of God in salvation and the eternal sweep of God's plan, by which believers are lifted from the depth of sin's depravity and curse to the heights of eternal joy and communion with God—by God's grace. That is what we have in chapters 1 and 2. Like 1 and 2 Corinthians and the pastoral letters, Ephesians deals with the church. But even more than those very practical letters, Ephesians shows how the church came into being, explains how it is to function, and gives guidelines for those important relationships in which the nature of the new humanity can be seen and by which it must grow.

Most Christians are aware of Paul's teaching about grace in chapter 2. In fact, many have probably memorized Ephesians 2:8-9: "For it is by grace you have been saved, through faith— and this not from yourselves, it is the gift of God—not by works, so that no one can boast." We will be looking at those verses in the next chapter. It is interesting, however, though not so widely recognized, that the word *grace* is used the same number of times and has an equally important place in chapter 1.

What is the difference between Ephesians chapters 1 and 2, since both are about salvation? The difference is that in chapter 1 Paul is looking at the matter from God's point of view, showing that we are saved because of what God has willed, and in chapter 2 he is looking at the same things from our perspective, showing how these prior decrees of God impact the believer.

But Paul begins with God!

A Golden Chain

The verses that deal with God's sovereign grace in salvation, Ephesians 1:3-14, are one long sentence in Greek, possibly the longest sentence in the New Testament. One commentator calls them "a magnificent gateway" to the epistle, another "a golden chain of many links," still another "an operatic overture and the flight of an eagle." But this long list of interconnected doctrines makes it hard to outline the section, and commentators have taken different approaches. John Stott gives them a temporal outline, speaking of the past blessing of election (vv. 4-6), the present blessing of adoption (vv. 7-8), and the future blessing of unification (vv. 9-10), followed by a section on the "scope" of these blessings. Others, such as E. K. Simpson and D. Martyn Lloyd-Jones, merely list the doctrines: focusing on such words as *election, adoption, redemption, forgiveness of sins, wisdom, unification in Christ,* and *the Holy Spirit.*

I think a Trinitarian outline is most helpful. Paul is saying that the blessings listed come from *God the Father* as a result of his electing choice, become ours in *Jesus Christ* by his work of redemption, and are applied to us by the *Holy Spirit* through what theologians term effectual calling. This is due to sovereign grace, since God is the subject of nearly every verb.

You can remember this outline by the acrostic ERA, not the Equal Rights Amendment or the soap powder with that name, but: "*E*lection," "*R*edemption," and "*A*pplication."

Elected by Sovereign Grace

The point at which Paul begins is the electing choice or predestining of God the Father. He writes,

> He chose us in him before the creation of the world
> to be holy and blameless in his sight. In love he pre-
> destinated us to be adopted as his sons through Jesus
> Christ, in accordance with his pleasure and will—to
> the praise of his glorious grace, which he has freely
> given us in the One he loves. (Eph. 1:4-6)

There are a lot of ideas in those verses, including such important ones as holiness, adoption, and the love of the Father for the Son. But the chief idea is election. It is introduced in several different ways:

Predestination is the technical word for election.

"In accordance with his pleasure and will" explains election as being by God's will only.

Grace is explicitly mentioned.

Finally, there are the words "which he has freely given." This is a further explanation of both grace and election.

These verses are one of the strongest expressions of sovereign grace in Scripture, for they teach that the blessings of salvation come to some people because God had determined from before the creation of the world to give these blessings to these people—and for that reason only. This is difficult for many persons to accept, of course. But the difficulties need to be worked through and overcome if grace is to be fully understood and appreciated.

One way people cope with the problem of election is to deny election outright. They will not deny that God was gracious in sending Jesus to be the world's Savior. He did not have to do it. Nor did Jesus have to die. But this is as far as they will go. They deny that people are saved because God has chosen to save them.

He offers salvation, but in the final analysis they are saved because they choose to receive Christ through their own free will. It is they who choose God, not God who chooses them.

This appeals to us, of course. We like to think of ourselves as being in control of our own destinies and being able to call the shots. But verses like these in Ephesians—and there are many more of them—say clearly that salvation is determined by God.

A second way of avoiding the truth of election is to admit the word but deny its effect by saying that the choice of God is based on foreknowledge. This is a mediating position taken by people who admit rightly that the Bible teaches election but who want to retain a commitment to human ability and perhaps also protect God from an act that seems to be unjust or arbitrary.

This is an impossible position, however. For one thing, an election based on foreknowledge of whether an individual will believe on God or not is not really election. It is the equivalent of saying that God chooses those who choose themselves. If that is the case, then the choice of the individual is obviously the critical choice, and the "choice" of God is in name only. It is actually only a response, and a compulsory one at that. In this approach God does not actually ordain anyone to anything.

An even more serious problem is that if what the Bible tells us about the spiritual inability and depravity of human nature is true, then there is nothing in man that God could possibly see on the basis of which he could elect to save him. The Bible teaches that: "There is no one righteous, not even one; there is no one who understands, no one who seeks God" (Rom. 3:10-11).

If that is correct, what could God possibly foresee as he looks down the long corridor of human history into the hearts of individuals except minds and moral dispositions radically opposed both to himself and grace. God cannot foresee something that cannot be. So even if God, in some sense, can be thought of as foreseeing faith in some persons, it can only be because he has determined in advance to put it there. And as a matter of fact, that is exactly what the next chapter of Ephesians teaches, that even faith is not from ourselves but "the gift of God" (Eph. 2:8).

When people have trouble with election—as many do—their real problem is not with election itself, though they suppose it is, but with the doctrine of depravity that makes election necessary.

The question to get settled first in any attempt to understand theology is this: When the human race fell into sin, how far did men and women fall?

Some people think that human beings fell upward. This is the view of evolutionists and many of today's humanists. They think mankind is getting better and better. Never mind that our cities are overwhelmed with crime, multiple brutal murders make every daily newspaper, television titillates us regularly with the latest sex offenses, especially by celebrities, and basic integrity is vanishing from Western life. Liberals can believe anything.

Other people suppose that man fell in some sense but that he did not fall the whole way. We might say that he fell onto a ledge where he has some small chance of climbing back onto the canyon edge. This is the view of Pelagians or Arminians (and probably most of today's American evangelicals). They admit sin's reality, but they deny its full effect. It's bad, but not so bad as to ruin the human race utterly. We may be disposed to evil, but not so much as to be incapable of repenting of sin and turning to Jesus Christ in faith when the gospel is made known to us. It does not require a miracle of grace, regeneration, to enable us to repent and believe on Jesus.

The only other view, the biblical one, is that when Adam and Eve sinned the human race fell the whole way. Human beings fell to the bottom of the ravine and cannot get out by their own power. "I've fallen down, and I can't get up" is the only accurate assessment of our spiritual condition. In fact, we are destined to remain down unless God on the basis of *his own sovereign choice* reaches out to perform the miracle of the new birth and thus lifts us up out of the pit of sin and sets us on the edge once again.

The Bible says that we are "dead in . . . transgressions and sins" (Eph. 2:1), and Jesus taught, "No one can come to me unless the Father who sent me draws him" (John 6:44).

In the declining days of the late Roman Empire, these issues were debated at length by a British monk named Pelagius and the great early church father Saint Augustine. Pelagius wanted to preserve human choice, as he saw it. He saw men and women as being formed more or less morally neutral. We make bad choices, he said. Bad choices dispose us to make further bad choices. But we do not need to make bad choices, and we always have the ability to turn ourselves back, repudiate our sins, and choose God. At one time Augustine thought like Pelagius. But he came to see, and then argued forcefully, that Pelagians do not do justice to the Bible's teachings about either sin or grace. They do not do justice to sin, because they try to preserve some little oasis, however small, of human goodness. They do not do justice to grace because a salvation that depends on human ability makes grace largely irrelevant. It is unnecessary. Besides, grace is no longer grace if it is based on something in human beings, either seen or foreseen.

Whenever I talk about election I like to point out that although it is problematic for some people, it is actually a doctrine filled with important blessings. Here are four of them.

1. Election eliminates boasting.

Critics of election often speak as if the opposite were true. They say that it is the height of arrogance for a person to claim that he or she has been chosen by God for salvation, as if that implies that there must be something special or worthy of praise about the chosen person. Election does not imply that at all. In fact, it is exactly the opposite. As I have been explaining, election has to do with God's choice only, entirely apart from anything that can be found in us. Look at Ephesians 1:4-6 again. They put the entire focus on God, making him the subject of each sentence. God "chose us" in Christ. "He predestined us to be adopted." "He has freely given us" all blessings. Moreover, all this is "to the praise of his glorious grace," not ours (v. 6). If any praise is due us, to exactly that degree glory is taken away from God and is given to man. It is only the pure doctrine of grace that keeps us humble.

2. Election gives assurance of salvation.

Suppose it were the other way around. Suppose that the ultimate ground of salvation is in ourselves. In that case, salvation would be as unsteady as we are since, if we can elect ourselves in, we can elect ourselves out. It is true, as we will see in the next study, that there are choices to make and things for us to do. But we are able to make these choices and do these good things only because God has first chosen us and made us to be new creatures. In fact, it is our security in his choice that is the basis for our action.

3. Election leads to holiness.

Ephesians chapter 1 also teaches this, for it says clearly that God "chose us . . . to be holy and blameless" (v. 4). In other words, election is not concerned only with the end result—that is, that we might be saved and go to heaven. It is also concerned with the steps along the way, which include holiness. Holiness is a direct result of God's determination since he has decreed that those who are being saved will be holy. If we are not growing in holiness, we are not elect. We are not saved persons.

4. Election promotes evangelism.

People have supposed that election must make evangelism unnecessary. "If God is going to save some person, then he will save that person regardless of what we may or may not do," they say. That does not follow. The fact that God determines the end does not mean that he ignores the means by which that end will be attained. He ordains the means, too. In this case, he has ordained that it is by means of preaching and teaching the Word that people will be converted.

Besides, it is only election that gives us any hope of success as we evangelize. If God cannot call people to faith effectively, how can we? We cannot persuade them. But if God is working, then he can work in us even if we are inept witnesses. We do not know who God's elect are, but we can find out who some of them are by telling them about Jesus. Those who are God's elect people will respond to our witness (or the witness of others), confess their sin, believe on Jesus, and grow in holiness. We can speak to them boldly because we know that God has promised to bless his Word and will not allow it to return to him without accomplishing his purpose (Isa. 55:11). We can know that all whom God has elected to salvation will be saved.

Redeemed by Sovereign Grace

Electing people to salvation is not the only thing God has done as an expression of sovereign grace. Following the Trinitarian pattern of this chapter, we come next to the doctrine of redemption. What God has done through Jesus Christ is to redeem his elect or chosen people (vv. 7-10). Redemption involves all three persons of the Godhead: (1) God the Father, who planned it; (2) God the Son, who accomplished it; and (3) God the Spirit, who applies it to God's people. But redemption is chiefly associated with Jesus, who is specifically called our Redeemer.

That is what our passage in Ephesians tells us. In verses 7 and 8, Paul is speaking of Jesus explicitly when he says, "In him [that is, in Jesus] we have redemption through his blood, the forgiveness of sins, in accordance with the riches of God's grace that he lavished on us with all wisdom and understanding."

The reason for this is that redemption is a commercial term meaning "to buy in the marketplace so that the object or person purchased might be freed from it," and Jesus did this for us by dying in our place. To carry the illustration out, we are pictured as slaves to sin, unable to free ourselves from sin's bondage and the world's grasp. Instead of freeing us, the world merely gambles for our souls. It offers everything that is its currency: fame, sex, pleasure, power, wealth. For these things millions sell their eternal souls and are perishing. But Jesus enters the marketplace as our Redeemer. Jesus bids the price of his blood, and God says, "Sold to Jesus for the price of his blood." There is no higher bid than that, and so we become his forever.

The apostle Peter wrote, "It was not with perishable things such as silver or gold that you were redeemed from the empty way of life handed down to you from your forefathers, but with the precious blood of Christ, a lamb without blemish or defect" (1 Pet. 1:18-19).

Charles Wesley was also describing God's sovereign grace in redemption when he wrote, using similar imagery,

> Long my imprisoned spirit lay
> Fast bound in sin and nature's night;
> Thine eye diffused a quick'ning ray,
> I woke, the dungeon flamed with light;
> My chains fell off, my heart was free,
> I rose, went forth and followed thee.

But here is a question for you. For whom did Jesus Christ die? Most people will respond, "For everyone, of course; Jesus died for the whole world," and there is a sense in which that is true. Jesus died for all kinds of people and for people scattered throughout the whole world. Also, his death has infinite value, being adequate to atone not only for the sins of all the people of this world but for all the sins of all the people of a billion worlds like this and more besides, if there are any. But that is not the question I am asking. I am asking, For whom did Jesus specifically die? That is, Whose sins did he actually atone for by his suffering?

Again, most people say that Jesus died for the sins of all persons and explain that all are not saved only because all will not believe on him. But the proper biblical answer is that Jesus died for the sins of his elect people only, the Father sending him to make specific atonement for the sins of those whom he had already elected to salvation. That is what Ephesians chapter 1 is saying. For the "we" who have been redeemed (v. 7) are the "us" who have been described earlier as being chosen and "predestined" to be saved (vv. 4-5).

Does it sound reasonable to say that Jesus died for all persons but that many are not saved only because they refuse to believe on Jesus? It may, at least until you think about the nature of that unbelief. Is their unbelief a morally neutral choice, just believing or not believing? Or is it a sin? The obvious answer is that unbelief is a sin, in fact, the most damning of all sins. But this means that if we really believe that Jesus died for all sins, then he must have died for this sin, too, and the result of this line of reasoning is that even the sin of unbelief will not keep a person out of heaven. This ends in universalism.

The greatest of all Puritan theologians was a scholar named John Owen. Few people read him today because his mind was so keen that most of today's sloppy thinkers cannot easily follow him. Owen was very sharp in this area. In a book titled *The Death of Death in the Death of Christ*, Owen argued that there are only three possible options where Christ's death is concerned. Either: (1) Christ died for all the sins of all men, so that all are saved, or (2) Christ died for all of the sins of some men, so that these but not all are saved, or (3) Christ died for some of the sins of all men. If it is the latter, then all are lost. They must perish for the sins for which Jesus did not die. The first is universalism, which Scripture rejects. The second is the correct and only biblical position.

To those who would argue that Jesus died for all the sins of all men but that all are not saved because all do not believe, Owen asked shrewdly, "This unbelief of theirs, is it a sin or is it not?" If it is not a sin, why should it keep them from salvation, since they cannot be condemned for an act that is not sinful? If we admit it is a sin, the question then becomes: Is it a sin for which Christ died, or is it not? If he did not die for it, then he did not die for all the sins of all men. If he did die for it, why should this more than any other sin for which he died keep an unbelieving person from salvation? Such clear thinking forces us back either to universalism, which we know to be wrong, or to the second or Calvinistic position.

The sovereign God has exercised his grace in salvation by sending Jesus to make specific atonement for his people's sins. In other words, grace expresses God's choice by what theologians call particular redemption.

Sealed by Sovereign Grace

The final expression of the sovereign grace of God emphasized in Ephesians 1 is the work of the Holy Spirit in applying the salvation thus planned by God the Father and achieved by God the Son to the individual (vv. 11-14).

At first glance the word *chosen* in verse 11 seems to be saying the same thing as Paul's words about the Father's choice in verse 4. But the idea is actually different. In verse 4 the predestining choice of the Father stands before everything. Here the choice made by the Holy Spirit follows predestination since the verse says that, "having been predestined according to [God's] plan," the Holy Spirit now makes God's electing choice effective in individual cases by choosing those individuals or leading them to faith. In other words, in verse 11, "chosen" refers to what theologians term the Holy Spirit's effectual call.

This effectual call is also because of sovereign grace.

The greatest picture of the grace of God calling a dead sinner to life in all the Bible is Jesus' raising of Lazarus, recorded in John 11. When Jesus got back to Bethany at the request of the dead man's sisters, he was told that Lazarus had been dead for four days and that he was already putrefying: "But Lord," said Martha . . . "by this time there is a bad odor, for he has been there four days" (v. 39). What a graphic description of the state of our moral and spiritual decay because of sin! There was no hope that anything could be done for Lazarus in this condition. His situation was not serious or grim; it was hopeless.

But only to man. Not to God. "With God all things are possible" (Matt. 19:26). Therefore, having prayed, Jesus called out, "Lazarus, come out!" (John 11:43), and the call of Jesus brought life to the dead man, just as the voice of God brought the entire universe into being from nothing at the beginning of the world.

That is what the Holy Spirit does today. The Holy Spirit works through the preaching of the Word of God to call to faith those whom God has previously elected to salvation and for whom Jesus Christ specifically died. Apart from those three actions—the act of God in electing, the work of Christ in dying, and the power of the Holy Spirit in calling—there would be no hope for anyone. No one could be saved. But because of those actions—because of God's sovereign grace—even the worst of blaspheming rebels may be turned from his or her folly and find the Savior.

Chapter 5

SALVATION BY GRACE ALONE

---

*Because of his great love for us, God, who is rich in
mercy, made us alive with Christ even when we were
dead in transgressions—it is by grace you have been
saved. . . . in order that in the coming ages he might
show the incomparable riches of his grace, expressed
in his kindness to us in Christ Jesus. For it is by grace
you have been saved. EPHESIANS 2:4-8*

The second chapter of Ephesians contains one of the best
known passages in the Bible, and rightly so. It contains the best
news that any woman or man can ever hear. With the exception
of John 3:16 and possibly Psalm 23, it is probably the Bible
passage that has been most memorized by Christians. John
wrote, "For God so loved the world that he gave his one and only
Son, that whoever believes in him shall not perish but have
eternal life" (3:16). Paul, in Ephesians 2:8-9, said the same thing
though in more theological language: "For it is by grace you have
been saved, through faith—and this not from yourselves, it is the
gift of God—not by works, so that no one can boast."

The verses have three parts.

Part one tells how God saves us. It is "by grace," the theme of this book.

Part two speaks of the channel through which the grace of God actually comes to us individually. It is "through faith."

Part three, a contrast, tells how God does *not* save us, and it explains why. It is "not by works, so that no one can boast."

Ephesians Chapters 1 and 2

Verses 8 and 9 are part of a great chapter, and the way to understand them, as well as to understand how we are "saved by grace," is to view them in this wider context. And part of that is to see chapter 2 in the context of the entire book of Ephesians.

A few years after I came to Philadelphia as pastor of Tenth Presbyterian Church, a committee met to review our Sunday school curriculum. We were unhappy with what we were using and also, for the most part, with what else was available. Either the curriculums were strong pedagogically but weak theologically, or else they were strong in Bible content and theology but weak in teaching. Chiefly we were disappointed by their failure to teach the great doctrines well. The result of our meeting was that in time we produced our own Sunday school material for the early grades. It followed a three-year cycle, repeated three times.

In the first year of this cycle basic doctrines were covered: sin, salvation, Bible study, prayer, and the Christian life.

In the second year the same areas were covered but from the perspective of the church and in terms of personal relationships. In this year, instead of talking about God providing salvation, we talked about the church, how one becomes a part of it, and how one is to act as a Christian.

The third year focused on God's view of history and the place of today's believers in that plan.

I mention our curriculum because there is a sense in which Paul does the same thing we did as he moves from the first to the second chapter of Ephesians, and later to the third and remaining chapters. We have already looked at Ephesians 1 in the last chapter, seeing how Paul presented the grace of God in salvation from the point of view of God, showing what each member of the Godhead did to save us: the Father chose us in Christ, the Son redeemed us from sin, the Holy Spirit applied that redemption to us by calling us to personal faith in Jesus. That is the picture in its grandest dimensions. Its goal is God's glory.

In chapter 2 this changes, for now Paul describes salvation from the perspective of the individual Christian. He shows what we were before the Holy Spirit called us to Christ, what God did for us in joining us to Christ, and what we are to become and do as a result.

The remaining chapters tell how Christians are to function in the world.

Here is another way of looking at it. Chapter 1 gives us the past, present, and future of God's great plan of salvation. Chapter 2 gives us the past, present, and future of the persons Jesus saves.

Speaking of past, present, and future reminds me of one of Harry Ironside's most delightful stories. Ironside was a Bible teacher, later pastor of Moody Memorial Church in Chicago. On this occasion he was riding on a train in southern California on the way to a speaking engagement. While he was sitting in the passenger car a gypsy came down the aisle offering to tell people's fortunes. She stopped at Ironside's seat, saying, "Cross my palm with a silver quarter, and I will tell your past, present, and future."

Ironside asked in an amused tone if she was sure she could do that, pointing out that he was of Scottish ancestry and did not want to part with a quarter unless he was sure he would get his money's worth. But she was very earnest. "Oh yes, sir," she said. "Cross my palm with a quarter, and I will tell you all."

Ironside told her this was not necessary because he already had his past, present, and future written down in a book. The gypsy was amazed. "In a book?" she queried.

"Yes," Ironside replied. "I have it with me." He pulled out his Bible and turned to these verses. "Here is my past," he said, reading Ephesians 2:1-3: "As for you, you were dead in your transgressions and sins, in which you used to live when you followed the ways of this world and of the ruler of the kingdom of the air, the spirit who is now at work in those who are disobedient. All of us also lived among them at one time, gratifying the cravings of our sinful nature and following its desires and thoughts. Like the rest, we were by nature objects of wrath."

The gypsy did not want to hear this. She began to pull away.

"Wait," said Ironside. "That is only my past. You haven't heard my present. Here it is." He began to read verses 4-6: "But because of his great love for us, God, who is rich in mercy, made us alive with Christ even when we were dead in transgressions— it is by grace you have been saved. And God raised us up with Christ and seated us with him in the heavenly realms in Christ Jesus."

At this point the gypsy was literally struggling to get away because Ironside had put his hand on her arm to hang onto her. "No more," she said. "I do not need to hear more."

But the preacher was not ready to quit. "You must hear my future too," he continued. He read verses 7-10: "in order that in the coming ages he might show the incomparable riches of his grace, expressed in his kindness to us in Christ Jesus. . . . For we are God's workmanship, created in Christ Jesus to do good works, which God prepared in advance for us to do."

By now the gypsy was heading rapidly down the aisle where she could be heard muttering, "I took the wrong man."

The Christian's Sad Past

Ironside was exactly right, of course. For the second chapter of Ephesians does give the past, present, and future of the Christian, showing how we have been brought out of a dismal past into a glorious present and bright future by the grace of God.

How are we to assess the Christian's past condition, that is, before he or she became a Christian? Paul says four things about it.

1. The sinner is "dead in . . . transgressions and sins."

In the entire history of the human race there have only been three basic views of man apart from God's grace, namely, to use three easy-to-understand terms, that man is: (1) well, (2) sick, or (3) dead.

The first view is that human beings are basically all right. It is the view of all optimists, which includes almost everyone today, at least where an evaluation of human nature is concerned. Optimists may vary as to how well they believe human beings are. Some would argue that people are very, very well. Others would admit that they are not as morally healthy as they may perhaps one day be. After all, there are still many problems in the world: wars, disease, starvation, poverty. But they would still say that the world is getting better and better, and the reason is that there is nothing basically wrong with man. He is evolving upward.

The second view is that man is not well. He is sick, even mortally sick, as some would say. This is the view of realists. They reject the optimistic view because they observe rightly that if people are as healthy as the optimists say, then surely the wars, disease, starvation, poverty, and other problems we wrestle with should have been fixed by now. Since they are not, they conclude that something is basically wrong with human nature. But still, the situation is not hopeless. Bad perhaps, even desperate. But not hopeless. People are still around, after all. They have not yet blown themselves off the surface of the planet or committed suicide by destroying the ozone layer or poisoning the world's oceans. Where there's life there's hope. There is no need to call the mortician yet.

The third view, the biblical view, which Paul articulates in classic language in this passage, is that man is neither well nor sick. Actually, so far as his relationship to God is concerned, he is dead, "dead in . . . transgressions and sins" (Eph. 2:1). That is, he is exactly what God had warned he would be before Adam and Eve's fall. Like a spiritual corpse, he is unable to make even a single move toward God, think a right thought about God, or even respond to God—unless God first brings this spiritually dead corpse to life so he can do it.

This is exactly what Paul says God does do in this passage.

2. The sinner is actively practicing evil.

There is something even worse about the biblical view of man, according to this passage. Human beings are spiritually dead, according to verse 1. But this is a strange kind of death since, although the sinner is dead, he is nevertheless up and about, actively practicing sin. What Paul says about him is that he "follow[s] the ways of this world and of the ruler of the kingdom of the air . . . gratifying the cravings of [his] sinful nature and following its desires and thoughts."

To put it differently, the sinner is indeed dead to God but nevertheless very much alive to all wickedness.

Some years ago I heard John Gerstner, a former professor at Pittsburgh Theological Seminary, compare Paul's description of our sinful state to what horror stories call a zombie. In case you are not up on zombie literature, let me explain that a zombie is a person who has died but who is still up on his feet walking around. It is a pretty gruesome concept, which is why it is in horror stories. But it gets worse. This upright, walking human corpse is also putrefying. It is rotting away. I suppose that is the most disgusting thing most people can imagine. But this is a fair description of what Paul is saying about human nature in its lost condition. Apart from Jesus Christ, these sinning human corpses are the living dead.

3. The sinner is enslaved.

Another way to speak of our active sinful state is to point out that men and women are enslaved to sin, so that they cannot escape from it. This seems to be another part of what Paul is describing in these verses. Enslaved to what? Well, there is a tradition in the church that identifies the Christian's three great enemies as the world, the flesh, and the devil. Paul seems to be saying here that in our natural state we are enslaved to each one.

We are enslaved to the world because we follow "the ways of this world" (v. 2). We think as the world thinks, with no regard for our relationship to God or our final destiny, and because we think as the world thinks, we act as the world acts, too. We are enslaved to the flesh because our natural desire is to "gratify . . . the cravings of our sinful nature and follow . . . its desires and thoughts" (v. 3). We want what we want, regardless of God's law or the effect that what we want and do has on other people. We are enslaved to the devil because just as we follow the ways of this world, so also do we follow "the ruler of the kingdom of the air, the spirit who is now at work in those who are disobedient" (v. 2). We are Satan's playthings, and never so much as when we are unaware even of his presence.

4. The sinner is by nature an object of God's "wrath."

This worst thing of all about our sinful condition is that, apart from God's grace in Jesus Christ, we are objects of God's wrath.

Most people can hardly take this seriously. "Wrath?" they say. "Did I hear you say wrath? You must be joking. I know people used to speak of God being angry with us because we do wrong things, but that is not the way to think of God today. Speak of God's love. Speak of mercy, even justice perhaps. But not wrath, at least not if you want to be taken seriously."

The outlook is an example of the very slavery about which I have just been writing. The world does not take wrath seriously because it does not take sin seriously. But if sin is as bad as the Bible (even this passage) declares it to be, then nothing is more reasonable than that the wrath of a holy God should rise against it. In the Old Testament there are more than twenty words that are used to express the idea of God's wrath, and more than six hundred important passages deal with it. In the New Testament there are two important words: *thumos*, which means "to rush along fiercely" or "be in a heat of violence," and *orge*, which comes from a root meaning "to grow ripe for something." The first word describes the release of the divine wrath in what we call the final judgment. It is found chiefly in Revelation, which describes this judgment. The second word points to God's gradually building an intensifying opposition to sin. It is the word found most often throughout the New Testament.

The Bible says, "'It is mine to avenge; I will repay,' and again, 'The Lord will judge his people.' It is a dreadful thing to fall into the hands of the living God" (Heb. 10:30-31).

The Christian's Present: Saved by Grace

The Christian's past is a dreadful thing, as it is also for all who have not believed on Jesus Christ. But at this point the grace of God comes in. For having spoken of the Christian's past, Paul now speaks of the Christian's present, saying,

> But [now] because of his great love for us, God,
> who is rich in mercy, made us alive with Christ
> even when we were dead in transgressions—it is by
> grace you have been saved. And God raised us up
> with Christ and seated us with him in the heavenly
> realms in Christ Jesus, in order that in the coming
> ages he might show the incomparable riches of his
> grace, expressed in his kindness to us in Christ
> Jesus. For it is by grace you have been saved."
> (Eph. 2:4-8)

This great "but" has changed everything. Left to ourselves, the cause was hopeless. But God has intervened to do precisely what needed to be done. We were dead in sins, but God has "made us alive with Christ." We were enslaved to sin, but God has "raised us up with Christ and seated us with him in the heavenly realms." That means we have been set free; there are no slaves in heaven. We were "objects of wrath," but God has made us objects of his overwhelming "grace."

That is the great word: *grace*. Grace alone.

During the last century, in one of the worst slum districts of London, there was a Christian social worker named Henry Moore-house. One evening as he was walking along the street he saw a little girl come out of a basement store carrying a pitcher of milk. She was taking it home. When she was just a few yards from Moore-house she suddenly slipped and fell. Her fingers relaxed their grip on the pitcher, and it crashed to the pavement and broke. The milk ran into the gutter, and the little girl began to cry as if her heart would break. Moorehouse stepped up to see if she was hurt. Then he helped her to her feet, saying, "Don't cry, little girl."

There was no stopping her tears, and she kept repeating, "My mommy'll whip me; my mommy'll whip me." Clearly this was a great tragedy for her.

Moorehouse said, "No, little girl, your mother won't whip

you. I'll see to that. Look, the pitcher isn't broken in many pieces." He stooped down beside her and began to work as if he were putting the pitcher back together. The little girl stopped crying. She had come from a family in which broken pitchers had been mended before. Perhaps this stranger could repair it. She watched as Moorehouse fitted several pieces together. But then, moving too roughly, he knocked the pieces apart once again, and this time she began to cry without stopping. She would not even look at the broken pieces lying on the sidewalk.

Suddenly the gentle Moorehouse picked the girl up in his arms and carried her down the street to a shop that sold crockery. He bought a new pitcher for her. Then, still carrying her, he went back to where the girl had bought milk and had the new pitcher filled. He asked where she lived. She told him, and he carried her to her house. Then, setting her down on the top step and placing the full pitcher of milk in her hands, he opened the door for her and asked as she stepped in, "Now, little girl, do you think your mother will whip you?"

He was rewarded for his trouble by a bright smile as she replied, "Oh, no, sir, 'cause it's a lot better pitcher 'an we had before."

This is a great illustration of the grace of God toward us in salvation! The Bible teaches that men and women were made in the image of God, as we saw in our first study. But when our first parents, Adam and Eve, sinned by eating of the forbidden tree, that image was broken beyond repair so far as pleasing God by any human effort was concerned. This does not mean that there is value to human nature from our point of view. Even a broken pitcher is not entirely without value. Archaeologists use broken pieces of pottery to date ancient civilizations. A shard can become an ashtray. Useful? Yes, a bit. But pottery that has been broken is worthless as far as carrying milk is concerned, just as human nature is worthless as a means of pleasing God.

But here is where grace comes in. In the story about Moorehouse, the little girl did not do anything to deserve the social worker's favor. She did not pay for her pitcher or hire him to help her. She did not even win over his sympathies because she was pretty or wretched or crying or pathetic. Moorehouse helped her only because it pleased him to do it. What is more, he didn't repair the pitcher. He gave her a new one, just as God gives us an entirely new nature when he makes us alive in Jesus Christ.

There is one more part of a Christian's present experience of God's grace that we need to mention here, and this is faith. We need to mention it because the text tells us that although we are saved by "grace alone," this grace nevertheless comes to us through the channel of human faith so that we can also speak of "faith alone."

At first glance this seems a contradiction. We want to ask, "How can salvation be by grace alone and by faith alone at the same time? If it is by grace alone, it can't also be by faith alone. If it is by faith alone, it can't be by grace." The problem is only a verbal one, however, and it vanishes as soon as we read the verses carefully. For what they teach—perhaps more clearly than any other passage in the Bible—is that faith is itself the result of God's gracious working. It is our faith. God does not believe for us. We believe. But we believe only because God has first enabled us to believe. Faith is there only because God has put it there. The text reads, "It is by grace you have been saved, through faith—*and this not from yourselves, it is the gift of God*—not by works, so that no one can boast" (vv. 8-9, italics mine).

The Christian's Bright Future

Having spoken of the Christian's past and present, the apostle now speaks of our future. This has two parts. There is a distant future, which Paul treats in verse 7, and there is an immediate future, which he treats in verse 10.

1. The distant future.

The Christian's distant future is that "in the coming ages [God] might show the incomparable riches of his grace, expressed in his kindness to us in Christ Jesus." We do not understand very much what this means because, as Paul wrote to the Corinthians, "No eye has seen, no ear has heard, no mind has conceived what God has prepared for those who love him" (1 Cor. 2:9). It is true that the very next verse adds, "but God has revealed it to us by his Spirit" (v. 10). But the context shows that at that point Paul is thinking of the mysteries of the gospel and not specifically of our future joy and blessings in heaven. What we can know is that, as God has been gracious to us here, so he will be continuously and exceedingly gracious to us in heaven forever. There is no good thing that he will ever withhold from those who are his people.

2. An immediate future.

The most interesting part of the Christian's future described here is what I have called our immediate future, which Paul refers to as doing "good works." And it is fascinating, too, because the verse immediately before this has said that it is "not by works" that we are saved. Not of works! Yet, created to do good works! Once again there seems to be a contradiction. But once again it is only an apparent contradiction. The true and important teaching is that, although we are not saved by works, being saved, we are nevertheless appointed by God to do them. If we think our good works have any part to play in our salvation, we are not saved. We are still in our sins. We cannot be saved by grace and be saved by grace plus works at the same time.

On the other hand, if we have been saved, we will not only want to do good works to please God who has been so gracious to us; we will actually do them. In fact, if we are not doing them, this is also a sign that we are not genuinely converted.

In my opinion, this is one of the most neglected, though

essential, teachings in the evangelical church in America today. The Protestant church is proud of its Reformation heritage in maintaining that we are saved by grace alone through faith alone. It repudiates the Catholic teaching that works combine with faith to produce justification. Protestants are right at this point. But Catholics are at least concerned to see works, and there are many segments of Protestantism that deny the place of works entirely. They teach that it is possible to be saved by faith alone and never produce any good works at all. They teach that it is possible to be saved but also to be utterly unchanged by that experience. What are we to say about a theology that does not have a place for works, especially in light of this important passage in Ephesians? What would Jesus think of such theology?

When we study Jesus' words, it does not take us long to discover that he insisted on changed behavior if a person was actually following him. He taught that salvation would be by his death on the cross. He said, "The Son of Man did not come to be served, but to serve, and to give his life as a ransom for many" (Mark 10:45). This is perfectly consistent with the fact of salvation by grace through faith alone, grace in his death and faith being our response to it.

But Jesus also said, "If anyone would come after me, he must deny himself and take up his cross daily and follow me" (Luke 9:23).

He said, "Why do you call me, 'Lord, Lord,' and do not do what I say? . . . The one who hears my words and does not put them into practice is like a man who built a house on the ground without a foundation. The moment the torrent struck that house, it collapsed and its destruction was complete" (Luke 6:46, 49).

He told the Jews of his day, "Unless your righteousness surpasses that of the Pharisees and the teachers of the law, you will certainly not enter the kingdom of heaven" (Matt. 5:20).

When we put these texts together it is easy to see that this is not only a matter of our demonstrating a genuinely changed behavior and thus doing good works if we are justified. It must also be that our good works exceed the good works of others, which is obvious once we consider that the Christian's good works flow from the character of God within the Christian. When Jesus said, "Unless your righteousness surpasses that of the Pharisees and the teachers of the law . . . ," he meant, "Unless you who call yourselves Christians, who profess to be justified by faith alone and therefore confess that you have nothing whatever to contribute to your own justification—unless you nevertheless conduct yourselves in a way which is utterly superior to the conduct of the very best people who are hoping to save themselves by their own good works, you will not enter God's kingdom because you are not Christians in the first place."

John Gerstner, whom I referred to earlier, has called this "a built-in apologetic" for Christianity. It is because no one but God could think up a religion like this. You and I would do it in either one of two ways. Either we would emphasize morality and end up saying that a person can justify himself by good works. Or else we would emphasize grace and teach that works do not matter, that it is possible to be saved by grace and yet be utterly unchanged. For us an emphasis on works leads to self-salvation. An emphasis on grace leads to antinomianism. But the true Christian religion, while it proclaims pure grace with no meritorious contribution from man mixed with it, nevertheless at the same time requires of Christians the highest possible degree of moral conduct.

Not for a moment can we suppose that there is anything we can do to earn or even contribute to our salvation. Salvation is truly and utterly by the grace of God alone. But if we are saved by that grace, that is, if we are who we claim to be as Christians, we will be abounding in good works lived by the new life of Christ within, works that glorify him.

Chapter 6

JUSTIFICATION BY GRACE ALONE

All have sinned and fall short of the glory of God, and
are justified freely by his grace through the redemption
that came by Christ Jesus. ROMANS 3:23-24

To start at the beginning, let me ask right off whether this chapter title, "Justification by Grace Alone," seems exactly right to you? If I had called it "Salvation by Grace Alone," the title of the last chapter, there would be no problem. We all know (or should know) that people are saved by God's grace only; it is what Ephesians 2 says clearly. Again, there would be no difficulty if I had called the chapter "Justification by Faith Alone." We know that phrase. It was the rallying cry of the Protestant Reformation, Martin Luther having called it the doctrine by which the church stands or falls.

But "Justification by Grace Alone"? Is that really right? Isn't it a confusion of terms?

The answer is that it is right, because it is only another way of saying what we are also saying by the other two statements. Salvation by grace alone, justification by grace alone, and justification by faith alone are really only three ways of stating the same great doctrine.

A full statement of the doctrine would be: "Justification by the grace of God alone received by faith alone, which is salvation."

Justification is an act of God as judge by which he declares us to be in a right standing before him so far as his justice is concerned. We are not just in ourselves. So the only way in which we can be declared to be in a right standing before God is on the basis of the death of Jesus Christ for our sins, he bearing our judgment, and by the application of Christ's righteousness to us by God's grace. This grace is received through the channel of human faith, but it is nevertheless by grace. It is the work of God, as we saw in our study of Ephesians chapter 1.

Justification by Grace

The text for this study is Romans 3:22-24, which says, "There is no difference, for all have sinned and fall short of the glory of God, and are justified freely by his grace through the redemption that came by Christ Jesus." This is the only place in this chapter where the word *grace* occurs, but it is important, if for no other reason than because it is the first theological treatment of grace in the New Testament.

I pointed out earlier that the word *grace* is mentioned not at all in Matthew or Mark, once in Luke, and only three times in John. It occurs eleven times in Acts, but these passages are not theological. So Romans is the first New Testament book to consider the word theologically, and this is the first theological treatment of the word in Romans. *Grace* occurs before this only in 1:5 and 7. In Romans there are twenty-one occurrences in all.

These verses are going to tell us how we are saved. But I want you to note that they begin by telling us that we need saving.

For a long time, whenever I came to Romans 3:23, I had the feeling that this verse was somehow in the wrong place. I did not think that Romans 3:23 was not true. Obviously it is. That is what chapters 1 and 2 and the first half of chapter 3 are about. They teach us that all have fallen short of God's standard. Even worse, we have rebelled against it and are moving off in the opposite direction as fast as possible. It was not that. It was rather that I felt that verse 23 really belonged in that earlier section, perhaps at the end of chapter 1 or in the first part of chapter 3. It seemed to me to have somehow gotten into the wrong place in this later section of the chapter, which talks about salvation.

It is not in the wrong place, of course; I see that now. And the reason is that without it we will not really understand or appreciate God's grace.

In one of his writings about grace Charles Haddon Spurgeon tells about a preacher from the north of England who went to call on a poor woman. He knew that she needed financial help. So with money from the church in his hand, he made his way through the poor section of the city where she lived, found her building, and climbed the four or five flights of stairs to her tiny attic apartment. He knocked at the door. There was no answer. He knocked again. Still no answer. Eventually he went away.

The next week he saw the woman in church and told her that he knew of her need and had been by to help her, but she was not at home.

"At what time did you call?" she asked.

"About noon," he said.

"Oh dear," she replied. "I was home and I heard you knocking. But I did not answer. I thought it was the landlord calling for the rent."

Spurgeon used that story as an illustration of grace, which it is. The preacher was trying to be gracious to the woman. But the reason I tell it here is to point out that we do not easily identify with the woman, though it is she in her need, rather than the preacher or anyone else, who actually represents our condition. As I told the story, isn't it true that you most naturally saw yourself in the position of the preacher, climbing the four or five flights of stairs, knocking at the apartment door and then going away? You did not identify with the woman. In fact, you may even have been laughing at her simplicity, which shows that you were thinking of her in a quite different category from yourself. She was unable to pay the rent. We know people like that. We feel sorry for them. But we do not believe that this is our condition. We can pay. We pay here, and we suppose we will be able to pay our proper share of the bills in heaven.

Or to change the interpretation slightly, we bar the door, but we do it for a different reason. We are not afraid that God is coming to collect the rent. On the contrary, we fear that he is coming with grace, and we do not want to be one who accepts a handout.

Someone was trying to explain the gospel to an upper-crust English lady on one occasion, stressing that every human being is a sinner. She replied with some astonishment, "But ladies are not sinners!"

"Then who are?" the Christian asked her.

"Just young men in their foolish days," was her answer.

Then the friend explained the gospel further, insisting that if she was to be saved, it would need to be by God's grace. She would have to be saved exactly as her footman needed to be saved—by the unmerited grace of God justifying her on the basis of Jesus' atonement.

She retorted, "Well, then, I will not be saved."

If you are to be justified by the grace of God, which is what this verse is about, then you must begin by understanding that you are in need of salvation and that, if you receive it, it will be entirely by grace. And that means that as far as your standing before God is concerned, there is no difference between you and any other sinner: "There is no difference, for all have sinned and fall short of the glory of God."

Is Etymology Helpful?

But what exactly is justification? We know it is important since, as I pointed out earlier, Martin Luther called it the doctrine by which the church stands or falls. John Calvin called it "the main hinge" upon which salvation turns. It was the chief doctrine of the Protestant Reformation. But what is it exactly? What does justification refer to?

One way to approach the meaning of theological terms is by etymology, that is, by the root meaning of the word or the word's parts. Unfortunately, that is not only unhelpful in this case, it is misleading. This is because justification is made up of two Latin words: *justus*, meaning "just," "fair," "equitable," or "proper," and *facio*, meaning "to make" or "to do." In English we use derivatives from the first word in the sphere of law, words like *just*, *justice*, and *justify*. The second word has given us such English words as *factory*, a place where things are made, and *manufacture*, which literally means "to make something by hand."

When we put these meanings together to explain justification, we get something like "to make just or righteous." But that is where the etymology becomes misleading. For justification does not mean "to be made righteous," as if it somehow changed our moral makeup or enabled us to live righteous lives. It actually means to have attained a right standing before the law. And in the case of our salvation, that is achieved, not by any change in us, but by the work of Jesus Christ, which is credited to us.

We can understand this by imagining that someone is brought before a judge owing a lot of money. He is about to suffer an adverse judgment in which his property will be forfeit. (In ancient times the individual could have been sold into slavery for debt.) But now a benefactor enters the judge's courtroom. "How much does my friend owe?" the new arrival asks.

"$350,000," says the judge.

"I'll pay that debt," says the friend. So it is done. The debt is paid, the papers are signed, and the judge dismisses the case. The defendant is now in a right standing before the law. He did not pay the debt himself, but it has been paid, and that is all the law requires. The man who was on trial is free to go. In the same way, Jesus pays our debt and so gives us a right standing before the bar of God.

Another way of saying this is to point out that justification is the opposite of condemnation. When a judge condemns a criminal, perhaps to prison, he is not turning the man into a criminal. He is only declaring in an official setting that the prisoner does not stand in a right relationship to the law and must therefore suffer the law's penalty. In the same way, justification does not mean that a sinner is somehow turned into one who is not a sinner, only that the sinner now stands in a right relationship to the law, and there is therefore now no penalty for that one. It is as Romans 8:1 states: "Therefore, there is now no condemnation for those who are in Christ Jesus."

But there is even more to justification than this. Justification is a two-part transaction. The first part is our sin being placed on Jesus Christ and being punished there, so that we do not have to be punished for it. The second part consists of his righteousness being placed to our account, so that we appear before God in his righteousness.

One of the great influences on my early life and ministry was Donald Grey Barnhouse, a former pastor of the church in Philadelphia I still serve. When Barnhouse was about fifteen years old, he heard the testimony of a man who had been a narcotics addict but who had been delivered from that life and had become a Christian minister. Barnhouse approached him and asked about his experience of Christ because he believed that the preacher had something he did not have, and the man gave him an object lesson that led to Barnhouse's conversion.

The man took Barnhouse's left hand, turned it palm upward, and then said intently, "This hand represents you." On it he placed a hymnbook, saying, "This book represents your sin. The weight of it is upon you. God hates sin, and his wrath must bear down against sin. Therefore, his wrath is bearing down upon you, and you have no peace in your heart or life." It was a telling statement, and Barnhouse knew it was true.

Then he took the young man's other hand and said, "This hand represents the Lord Jesus Christ, the Savior. There is no sin upon him, and the Father must love him, because he is without spot or blemish. He is the beloved Son in whom the Father is well pleased." There were Donald's two hands, the one weighted down by the large book, the other empty. Again he knew it was true. He had the sin. Jesus had none.

Then the older teacher put his hand under Barnhouse's left hand and turned it over so that the book now came down upon the hand that earlier had been empty. He put the left hand back, its burden now transferred to the hand that stood for Jesus. He said, "This is what happened when the Lord Jesus Christ took your place on the cross. He was the Lamb of God, bearing away the sin of the world."

While the hymnbook representing Barnhouse's sin still rested upon the hand representing Jesus Christ, the preacher turned to his Bible and began to read verses that taught what he had illustrated:

First, 1 Peter 2:23-24: "When they hurled their insults at him, he did not retaliate; when he suffered, he made no threats. Instead, he entrusted himself to him who judges justly. He himself bore our sins in his body on the tree, so that we might die to sins and live for righteousness."

Then, Isaiah 53:4-6, the verses to which Peter was referring:

> Surely he took up our infirmities and carried our sor-
> rows, yet we considered him stricken by God, smit-
> ten by him, and afflicted. But he was pierced for our
> transgressions, he was crushed for our iniquities; the
> punishment that brought us peace was upon him,
> and by his wounds we are healed. We all, like sheep,
> have gone astray, each of us has turned to his own
> way; and the LORD has laid on him the iniquity of us
> all.

The preacher stopped reading and addressed the young man directly. "Whose sins were laid on Jesus?" he asked.

"Our sins," he replied.

"Whose sins does that mean?" the preacher probed.

"Our sins," came the same answer.

"Yes, but whose sins are those?"

"Well, everybody's sins—your sins, my sins . . ."

The older man interrupted and caught the words almost before they were out of Barnhouse's mouth. "*My* sins; yes, that's it," he said. "That's what I want. Say it again."

Barnhouse obeyed. "My sins," he repeated.

The preacher then went back to Isaiah 53:6. He put the hymn-book back on Barnhouse's left hand and pressed down upon it as he read, "We all, like sheep, have gone astray, each of us has turned to his own way." The pressure was strong. But then he turned the book and hand over once again, so that the burden was transferred to the hand that represented Jesus Christ, and he continued his reading: "and the LORD has laid on him the iniquity of us all."

Barnhouse understood it then, and he never forgot it. In fact, he used that same illustration to teach many others about justification and lead them to the Savior.

He expanded it, too. For just as the transfer of the hymn-book showed the transfer of our sins to Jesus, where they have been punished, so also is it possible to show the transfer of the righteousness of Jesus Christ to us by a movement in the opposite direction, since a double transfer is involved.

The second side of the transfer is presented in Romans 3 in the verse immediately before our text. It says, "This righteousness from God comes through faith in Jesus Christ to all who believe" (v. 22). In the following chapter it is explained in the case of David who, we are told, "says the same thing when he speaks of the blessedness of the man to whom God credits righteousness apart from works" (Rom. 4:6), and in the case of Abraham who "is the father of all who believe but have not been circumcised, in order that righteousness might be credited to them" (Rom. 4:11).

Horatio G. Spafford celebrated the first half of the transaction when he composed these lines:

> My sin—oh, the bliss of this glorious thought,
> My sin—not in part, but the whole,
> Is nailed to the cross, and I bear it no more,
> Praise the Lord,
> Praise the Lord, O my soul!

Count von Zinzendorf was thinking of the second half when he wrote:

> Jesus, thy blood and righteousness
> My beauty are, my glorious dress;
> 'Midst flaming worlds, in these arrayed,
> With joy shall I lift up my head.

By Faith Alone

Thus far, our study of justification has shown that the source of our justification is the grace of God and that the ground of our justification is the work of Christ. The first point is made in Romans 3:24 ("justified freely by his grace"), the second point in

Romans 3:25 ("God presented him as a sacrifice of atonement"). There is one more point that needs to be made, namely, the channel of our justification is faith. This is taught in verse 25 also ("through faith in his blood"), but references to faith as the means of justification are actually found throughout this section. There are eight occurrences of the word *faith* in verses 21-31.

What is faith? There are many wrong or misleading definitions of faith, like "believing what you know ain't so" or positive thinking ("I can because I think I can"). But we do not need to spend time on those. The best way to define faith is to think of it as having three parts. Some writers have called these "awareness, assent, and commitment" or "knowledge, belief, and trust." In the classical theology of the Reformation and post-Reformation period, they were described by three Latin words: *notitia*, *assensus*, and *fiducia*. The first has to do with content, the second with a believing response to that content, the third with commitment.

1. Faith involves content.

The first important thing to be said about the faith through which we are justified is that it involves knowledge of the truth of the gospel or what I call *content*. Faith always has content. Faith without content is not true faith at all.

John Calvin was very strong on this point because during the Middle Ages an error about faith had developed that almost destroyed the meaning of true faith and with it true Christianity. In the hundreds of years before the Reformation the church had failed to teach the Bible to its people, and as a result very few people had any real understanding of the gospel. Most of the clergy were ignorant of it also. How, then, were such ignorant people to be saved? The answer given was that it was by an "implicit" faith. That is, it was not necessary for any particular communicant actually to know anything. It was the church that understood the truth. All that was necessary was that the church-going person trust the church implicitly. All he had to believe was that the church was right and that he would be saved so long as he trusted the church, whatever its actual teachings were.

The situation that developed in the Middle Ages reminds me of a man who was being interviewed by a group of church officers before being taken into membership. They wanted to know what he believed about the gospel, and he replied that he believed what the church believed.

This did not satisfy the officers. So they asked, "What does the church believe?"

"The church believes what I believe," the man answered.

The committee was getting frustrated, but the officers tried one final time. "And just what do you and the church believe?" they probed.

The man thought for a moment, then answered, "We believe the same thing."

This is exactly the way faith had come to be understood in the years before the Reformation, and it was this that Calvin attacked. He argued, as did the other reformers, that true faith must rest on a right knowledge of the gospel. Otherwise, he said, it is just pious ignorance. We are not saved by abandoning our mind to some external authority. Rather, we must know what we believe and build on it.

2. Faith involves assent to the Bible's teaching.

It is easy to understand why this is a necessary second part of true faith, for we can see at once that it is possible to understand something and yet not believe it personally. When I was a student at Harvard University studying English literature, I had a number of professors who understood the central doctrines of Christianity better than a majority of ministers. Doctrines such as the nature of God, the deity of Christ, the blood atonement, sin, repentance, and faith pervade English literature, and the professors who were teaching in the department had mastered the doctrines in order to understand the literature. But they didn't believe them. They regarded them as an historical curiosity, on the same level as the Ptolemaic system of astronomy, alchemy, the medieval theory of bodily humors, or any other such thing.

So faith is more than merely understanding the Bible's doctrines. It also requires assent to those doctrines, which is why the Reformation and post-Reformation theologians added the word *assensus* to *notitia*. *Notitia* is like our word *notice*. It involves information only. *Assensus* adds the idea of assenting to it. It means saying, "I believe this is true."

This step is also more than just cold intellectual assent, at least for most people. This is because the truths believed are not abstract truths that hardly concern us, like some mathematical proof or the calculation of the position of a star in astronomy. They concern the nature and work of God and his great love for us, which he has demonstrated by sending his Son Jesus Christ to die for our salvation.

> He saw me ruined in the fall
> And loved me not withstanding all;
> He saved me from my lost estate:
> His loving kindness, oh, how great!

Nobody can really believe that and not be moved by it, at least in some way. When John Wesley reached this point in his spiritual pilgrimage, as he did in responding to the reading of Martin Luther's preface to Romans in that famous meeting in the chapel in Aldersgate Street in London, he described his experience by saying that his heart was "strangely warmed." It was the point at which his spirit assented to the truths of the gospel that he had understood, but only intellectually understood, for years.

3. Faith involves commitment.

The last part of faith is commitment to the one who loved us and died for us. It is of critical importance simply because it is possible to understand these truths, believe they are true, and yet pull back from the necessary commitment that will actually enlist us as one of Christ's followers. There are people who teach that it is possible to be a Christian, to be saved by faith, and yet not be committed to Jesus in this way. The answer to this error is to point to the devil, who knows the doctrines of the gospel and believes they are true, but who certainly has not committed himself to follow Christ.

James was speaking of this false faith, contrasting it with true faith, when he wrote that the devils also "believe" but "shudder" (James 2:19).

Which leads me to the best of all illustrations of faith, the way in which a young man and a young woman meet, fall in love, and get married. The first stages of their courtship correspond to the first element in faith, which has to do with content. That is, they are getting to know one another to try to see if the other person is the kind of person to whom they would like to be married. The second stage is what we call falling in love. It corresponds to assent, especially the warming of the heart. We think very highly of this stage, and rightly so. But even it does not constitute a marriage. The marriage takes place only when the couple stand before the minister and exchange their vows, thus formalizing their commitment to one another.

So also in salvation. Jesus makes his commitment to us. He says, "I, Jesus, take thee, sinner, to be my true disciple and bride; and I do promise and covenant, before God the Father and these witnesses, to be thy loving and faithful Savior and Lord; in plenty and in want, in joy and in sorrow, in sickness and in health, for this life and for all eternity."

And the time comes when we look up into his face and say, "I, sinner, take thee, Jesus, to be my Savior and Lord; and I do promise and covenant, before God and these witnesses, to be thy loving and faithful disciple, in plenty and in want, in joy and in sorrow, in sickness and in health, for this life and for all eternity." Then God the Father, not an earthly minister, pronounces the marriage, and you or I become the bride of Jesus Christ forever.

Have you made that commitment? If not, this is the place to do it. I have written a great deal about grace. But wonderful as grace is, it will do you no good until by faith you become a follower of Jesus Christ. In this study I have talked about justification. But justification is by the grace of God *through faith*. You must commit yourself to Jesus.

Chapter 7

STANDING IN GRACE

Through whom we have gained access by faith into this grace in which we now stand. ROMANS 5:2

Have you heard this classic put-down of someone who has been acting arrogantly? "If you're so smart, why aren't you rich?"

I think of it as we move from Romans 3 to Romans 5 because I know that a person might read what I have written about justification by grace and ask: "If justification is as great as you say it is, why aren't *Christians* rich?" The answer, of course, is that Christians are rich, spiritually. It is what the fifth chapter of Romans is about. Romans 5 tells us that our standing in grace has swelled our spiritual assets by giving us: (1) peace with God, (2) union with Christ, (3) a transformed response to suffering, and (4) a confident hope of our ultimate glorification.

Standing in *This* Grace

Romans 5:2 is the pivotal verse for understanding these benefits of justification, but it is not easy to understand, since its key words—*access, faith, grace,* and *standing*—can all be used in different ways. It is not immediately clear how they go together in this sentence. So we should begin by defining each of these key words:

1. Grace.

Grace is "God's unmerited favor," sometimes rightly strengthened to read "God's favor to those who actually deserve the opposite." In this sense, grace is what lies behind God's plan of salvation. That is why Paul can use it in writing to the Ephesians, saying, "For it is by grace you have been saved, through faith—and this not from yourselves, it is the gift of God—not by works, so that no one can boast" (Eph. 2:8-9).

But this is not the precise meaning of the word *grace* in Romans 5:2. One clue that Paul is giving *grace* a slightly different meaning is that he prefaces it with the word *this*. "*This* grace!" It indicates that he has a specific grace in mind. Another clue is that Paul speaks of it as the grace "in which we now stand." What grace is it in which we now stand? In the context of Romans, it is clear that it is our state of justification. It means that, while before we were "under wrath," now we are "under grace" if we stand before God as justified men and women.

2. Faith.

Faith also has a variety of meanings. It always means "believing God and acting upon that belief." But the emphasis can be upon our conduct (being faithful), believing (taking God at his word) or what we are called upon to believe (the faith once delivered to the saints). Since faith is linked to the words *this grace* and since this is the grace of justification, the faith referred to here must be the faith in Jesus Christ through which we are justified.

3. *Access.*

The Greek term lying behind this word is *prosagogē*, which means "right to enter," "freedom to enter" or "introduction." Since it is used of the work of the Holy Spirit in prayer in Ephesians 2:18, it has been said sometimes that the Holy Spirit "introduces" us to God.

The important thing to see about its use in Romans 5:2 is that it is preceded by the verb "have gained" and that this verb is in the past perfect tense. The New International Version reads "have gained" to emphasize this tense. But the word is actually *have*, and in the past perfect tense the proper translation is "have had." Paul is saying that we "*have had* our access into the grace of justification.*" Paul uses this special past tense to show that the justification in which we stand is something that has been accomplished for us and into which we have already entered.

It has a present significance, too. But the reason it has a present significance is that it is something that has already happened to us. We have been justified; therefore we remain justified. We have had our access, and it is because we have had it that we still have it.

4. *Stand.*

The final key word of Romans 5:2 is *stand*. By now we can see how it should be taken. By the mercy of God we have been brought into the grace of justification, and that is the grace in which we now have the privilege to stand. Before we were standing outside the sphere of God's blessing, as children of wrath. Now we are standing within that sphere, as sons and daughters of God. The point is that we have been made secure in Christ, and that forever. We have entered into grace and now stand in grace with an entirely different status than we had before.

Peace with God

This new state has several important features marked by the other key words in the first half of Romans 5. The first is *peace*. It occurs in verse 1 in the phrase "peace with God."

This is a military metaphor, and it points to the fact that before our justification we were not at peace with God. We might say, as Henry David Thoreau is quoted as having said, "I am not at war with God." But we are lying when we say that. Jesus said that our responsibility is to "love the Lord your God with all your heart and with all your soul and with all your mind," and that the second is to "love your neighbor as yourself" (Matt. 22:37, 39; cf. Deut. 6:5; Lev. 19:18). But we do not love God in our unsaved state. We actually hate God, hate others, and hate ourselves. Someone has said that we would murder God if we could, we murder others when we can, and we commit spiritual suicide every day of our lives.

However, having been justified by grace through faith in Jesus Christ, this state of spiritual warfare has been changed to one of peace. We now have peace with God, make peace with others, and experience a new measure of personal peace within ourselves.

Yet it is not only that we are at war with God in our natural state. God is also at war with us because of our ungodly behavior (cf. Rom. 1:18). The word Paul has been using is *wrath*, saying that "the *wrath* of God is being revealed from heaven against all the godlessness and wickedness of men who suppress the truth by their wickedness" (v. 18, italics mine). Having shown what this means and having answered the objections of those who feel that this may be a right description of the condition of other people, but not of themselves, Paul reveals what God has done to satisfy his wrath against us in Jesus Christ. Christ bore the Father's wrath in our place. He died for us, and we receive the benefits of his atonement by believing on him and in what he has done. This is what we were studying in the last chapter.

But where does this lead? Obviously to peace with God. For since we have been justified by faith, the cause of the conflict is removed and peace is the result. Peace has been provided from God's side, for God has removed the cause of the enmity through Jesus' death. Peace has been received on our side, for we have "believed God" and have found the righteousness of the Lord Jesus Christ to be credited to us as our righteousness.

Union with Christ

The second benefit of standing in the grace of justification is union with Christ, which is discussed extensively in the second half of Romans 5, though it is found in these earlier verses as well. Verses 1-11 teach that justification is important—immensely important. But in addition the passage also teaches that we are united to Christ in what theologians call "the mystical union." This means a union with Christ that we do not fully understand but that God has revealed to us.

Paul mentions this first in verse 10, which speaks of our being "saved through his life!" In the Greek text the last three words are "*in* his life." So the argument is: If God has saved us through the death of Christ (through faith in his atonement), he will certainly save us by our being "in him."

Here are two important points to keep in mind.

First, the union of the believer with Christ is one of three great unions in Scripture. The first is the union of the persons of the Godhead in the Trinity. Christians, just as much as Jews, speak of one God. Yet on the basis of the revelation of God in Scripture, we also believe that this one God exists in three persons as God the Father, God the Son, and God the Holy

Spirit. We cannot explain how these three persons of the God-head are at the same time only one God, but the Bible teaches this and we believe it.

The second mystical union is of the two natures of Christ in one person. The Lord Jesus Christ is one person. Nevertheless, he is also both man and God, possessing two natures. The theological formulation of this truth at the Council of Chalcedon (A.D. 451) said that Jesus is

> to be acknowledged in two natures, inconfusedly,
> unchangeably, indivisibly, inseparably; the distinc-
> tion of natures being by no means taken away by
> the union, but rather the property of each nature
> being preserved, and concurring in one Person and
> one Subsistence, not parted or divided into per-
> sons, but one and the same Son.

If you understand that completely, you are a better theologian than I am. But although I do not fully understand it, I believe it since it seems to be what the Bible teaches.

In the case of the union of believers with Christ, we may never fully understand this relationship either. But it is an important truth, and we should hold onto it and try to gain understanding.

Second, the mystical union of the believer with Christ is not something that was invented by the church's theologians or even by the apostle Paul but rather was first taught by Jesus and then was built upon by Paul. Jesus taught it by analogies, which also occur again later in Scripture. Let me list a few.

1. The vine and the branches.

Jesus said,

> I am the true vine. . . . Remain in me, and I will
> remain in you. No branch can bear fruit by itself; it
> must remain in the vine. Neither can you bear fruit

> unless you remain in me. I am the vine; you are the
> branches. If a man remains in me and I in him, he
> will bear much fruit; apart from me you can do
> nothing. (John 15:1, 4-5)

The emphasis in these verses is upon the nourishing power of Christ working itself out through his disciples. Paul builds on this image when he speaks of the "fruit of the Spirit" (Gal. 5:22-23).

2. The Lord's Supper.

On the same evening that Jesus spoke about himself as the vine and his disciples as the branches, he gave instructions for observing the Lord's Supper, saying, "This is my body" and "This is my blood of the covenant" (Matt. 26:26, 28). The elements symbolize our participation in the life of Christ. In the same way Jesus discoursed on the bread of life, saying, "I am the bread of life. He who comes to me will never go hungry, and he who believes in me will never be thirsty" (John 6:35). He also challenged the woman of Samaria with the words, "Everyone who drinks this water will be thirsty again, but whoever drinks the water I give him will never thirst. Indeed, the water I give him will become in him a spring of water welling up to eternal life" (John 4:13-14).

The emphasis in this image is on our becoming so closely joined to Jesus that he is as much a part of us as something we eat.

3. A foundation and the structure built upon it.

Jesus introduced this image when he spoke of himself as the right foundation for building a life:

> Everyone who hears these words of mine and puts
> them into practice is like a wise man who built his
> house on the rock. The rain came down, the

> streams rose, and the winds blew and beat against
> that house; yet it did not fall, because it had its
> foundation on the rock. (Matt. 7:24-25)

Paul added to this image when he told the Christians at Corinth, "You are . . . God's building. . . . No one can lay any foundation other than the one already laid, which is Jesus Christ" (1 Cor. 3:9, 11) and when he wrote to the Ephesians, "You are no longer foreigners and aliens, but fellow citizens with God's people and members of God's household, built on the foundation of the apostles and prophets, with Christ Jesus himself as the chief cornerstone" (Eph. 2:19-20). In the next verse the building becomes a temple: "In him the whole building is joined together and rises to become a holy temple in the Lord" (v. 21). It is only because we are "in Christ" that this is possible.

This image shows that, being joined to Christ, we are at the same time also joined to one another. We are part of the church.

4. The head and members of the body.

This was one of Paul's favorite images. "God placed all things under his [Christ's] feet and appointed him to be head over everything for the church, which is his body, the fullness of him who fills everything in every way" (Eph. 1:22-23). Again,

> He . . . gave some to be apostles, some to be proph-
> ets, some to be evangelists, and some to be pastors
> and teachers, to prepare God's people for works of
> service, so that the body of Christ may be built
> up. . . . Then we will no longer be infants, tossed
> back and forth by the waves, and blown here and
> there by every wind of teaching and by the cunning
> and craftiness of men in their deceitful scheming.
> Instead, speaking the truth in love, we will in all
> things grow up into him who is the Head, that is,

Christ. From him the whole body, joined and held together by every supporting ligament, grows and builds itself up in love, as each part does its work. (Eph. 4:11-12, 14-16)

In these verses the emphasis is upon two things: (1) growth, and (2) the proper functioning of the church under Christ's direction. In 1 Corinthians Paul uses this image to show that each individual Christian is needed if the church is to function properly (cf. 1 Cor. 12:12-27).

5. Marriage.

The greatest of all illustrations of the union of the believer with Christ and of Christ with the believer is marriage. It is found in the Old Testament, in Hosea, for example, where God compares himself to the faithful husband who is deserted by Israel, the unfaithful wife. Jesus used it when speaking of a marriage supper to which guests are invited (Matt. 22:1-14). Paul develops it in what is probably the best known passage from Ephesians, mixing it with the image of the church as Christ's body.

Wives, submit to your husbands as to the Lord. For the husband is the head of the wife as Christ is the head of the church, his body, of which he is the Savior. Now as the church submits to Christ, so also wives should submit to their husbands in everything. Husbands, love your wives, just as Christ loved the church and gave himself up for her to make her holy, cleansing her by the washing with water through the word, and to present her to himself as a radiant church, without stain or wrinkle or any other blemish, but holy and blameless. In this same way, husbands ought to love their

wives as their own bodies. . . . This is a profound
mystery—but I am talking about Christ and the
church. (Eph. 5:22-28, 32)

In this doctrine we are dealing with our security in Christ. But
the question we must ask ourselves is: Am I really in Christ? Am
I a Christian?

How can you know? Use the marriage illustration. Ask yourself: Am I married to Jesus? If you have taken the vow, promising
to "take Jesus to be your loving and faithful Savior, in plenty and
in want, in joy and in sorrow, in sickness and in health, for this
life and for eternity," and if you are living for him, you are. God
has solemnized the marriage, and what God has joined together
no one will ever put asunder.

Joy in Suffering

You have probably heard the tired atheistic rebuttal to Christian
doctrine based upon the presence of suffering in the world. One
form of it goes like this: "If God were good, he would wish to
make his creatures happy, and if God were almighty he would be
able to do what he wished. But his creatures are not happy.
Therefore God lacks either goodness or power or both." That
objection is insulting in its simplicity, for it assumes that absence
of suffering is the only ultimate good and that the only possible
factors involved in our quandary are the alleged benevolence and
alleged omniscience of God. The Christian *knows* that there is
more to suffering than this.

Still, the problem of suffering is a big one, and coping with it
is not always easy. How should Christians respond to their trials?
How can their response strengthen confidence that they are truly
converted persons?

Paul says that because Christians stand in grace they are able to respond to their trials by rejoicing in them, however strange, abnormal, or irrational this may seem to unbelievers, and that this is another evidence of their salvation. His exact words are: "Not only so, but we also rejoice in our sufferings, because we know that suffering produces perseverance; perseverance, character; and character, hope. And hope does not disappoint us, because God has poured out his love into our hearts by the Holy Spirit, whom he has given us" (Rom. 5:3-5).

Each of the major words in these verses is important, but if someone should ask, "What is the most important word?" I would answer that it is the word *know* in verse 3. The phrase reads, "because we know . . ." *Know* is important because knowledge is the secret to everything else in the sentence. Christians rejoice in suffering because of what they know about it. These verses state several important truths they know.

1. Suffering produces perseverance.

You may notice another word used to translate this idea in your Bible—if you are using one other than the New International Version—because the word seems to most translators to call for a richness of expression. Some versions say, "patience," others, "endurance," still others, "patient endurance."

The full meaning emerges when we consider it together with the word for "suffering," which occurs just before it in the Greek text and which is the thing Paul says produces "patience." There are a number of words for suffering in the Greek language, but this one is *thlipsis*, which has the idea of pressing something down. It was used for the effect of a sledge threshing grain, for instance. The sledge pressed the stalks down and thus broke apart the heads to separate the chaff from the grain. *Thlipsis* was also used for the crushing of olives to extract their oil or of grapes to press out wine.

With that in mind, think now of "perseverance." The word

translated "perseverance" is *hypomon*. The first part of this word is a prefix meaning "under" or "below." The second part is a word meaning an "abode" or "living place." So the word as a whole means "to live under something." If we take this word together with the word for tribulation, we get the full idea, which is to live under difficult circumstances without trying, as we would say, to wriggle out from under them. We express the idea positively when we say, "Hang in there, brother." It has to do with "hanging tough" when the going gets tough, as it always does sooner or later.

This separates the new Christian from one who has been in the Lord's school longer. The new believer tries to avoid difficulties and get out from under them. The experienced Christian is steady under fire and does not quit his post.

2. Suffering produces character.

Other versions translate this word "experience." But it is richer even than these two good renderings. The Greek word is *dokim*, which is based on the adjective *dokimos*, meaning something "tested" or "approved." It suggests this image.

In the ancient world silver and gold coins were roughly made, not milled to exact sizes as our coins are, and people would often cheat by carefully trimming off some of the excess metal. We know they did this because hundreds of laws were passed against defacing coins. After they had trimmed away enough metal, the people would sell them for new coins, and when coins had been trimmed for a long time, they eventually got so light that merchants would no longer take them. When that happened, the coins were said to be *adokimos*, "disqualified."

"Disqualified" is a negative form of what Paul is referring to in Romans 5. He is saying that the pressures of trying to live for Jesus in this world produce endurance that proves we are qualified to be his servants.

I think of it this way, too. A disapproved coin is a light coin, and we become spiritually "light" when we draw away from God. We become more and more weightless. But when we suffer and therefore draw close to God and he also to us, we become spiritually and morally weighty, as he is.

Ray Stedman tells of a time he once asked a nine-year-old boy, "What do you want to be when you grow up?"

The boy said, "A returned missionary."

He did not want to be just a missionary, but a returned one—one who had been through the fires, had them behind him, and was shown to have been of value in God's work.

3. Suffering produces hope.

Hope means confident expectation of our final glorification, as in "hope of the glory," the phrase with which we will end (v. 2). It is further evidence of our new status in Christ since it proves that we are identified with him.

Some years ago Dr. Jonathan Chao gave an address on the suffering of Christians in China, showing that it was the suffering of the church that produced its character. He told of an American student who came to Hong Kong to study the Chinese church. Before he had left America a friend had asked him, "If God loves the Chinese church so much, why did he allow so much suffering to come upon it?" The student confessed that he had no answer at the time. But after he had traveled to China and had made extensive and meaningful contacts with a number of Chinese Christians, he discovered an answer, which he put like this: "I am going back to America and ask my friend this question: If God loves the American church so much, why hasn't he allowed us to suffer like the church in China?"

It was a good answer since, according to the Bible, suffering is not a harmful but a beneficial thing. It is beneficial because it accomplishes the beneficent purposes of almighty God. It is part

THE GLORY OF GOD'S GRACE

of those circumstances all of which work "for the good of those who love him" (Rom. 8:28).

Hope of Glory

Paul wrote the fifth chapter of Romans to teach those who have been justified by God through faith in Jesus Christ that they are secure in their salvation. We have already seen several ways he has done this. He has spoken of the "peace" that has been made between God and ourselves by the work of Christ, our mystical union with Christ, and the different way you and I are able to regard suffering because of our knowledge of what God is doing with us.

Paul spoke of "the hope of the glory of God." By this term, he meant our glorification, our ultimate destiny as believers. So the phrase is an anticipation of the statement in Romans 8:30: "And those he predestined, he also called; those he called, he also justified; those he justified, he also glorified." Justification leads to glorification because if God has justified us, he will also glorify us.

Here are two important points about glorification.

First, this glorious culmination of our salvation by God is certain. We have seen many facets of this throughout this book, but it is necessary to emphasize it here especially because of Paul's use of the word *hope*. In our day *hope* is a weak word. The dictionary defines it pretty well with the words: "desire with expectation of obtaining what is desired," "trust," "reliance." But in common speech we usually mean much less than this. We speak of "hoping against hope" or "hoping for the best," which means we are not really very hopeful.

This is not what hope means in the Bible. In the Bible hope is a certainty, and the only reason it is called hope rather than certainty is that we do not possess the thing that is hoped for yet, though we will. Here are some examples of how *hope* is used.

> Acts 2:26-27—"My body . . . will live in hope, because you will not abandon me to the grave."

> 1 Corinthians 13:13—"These three remain: faith, hope and love."

> 2 Corinthians 1:7—"Our hope for you is firm."

> Colossians 1:27—"Christ in you, the hope of glory."

> Titus 1:2—"Hope of eternal life, which God, who does not lie, promised before the beginning of time."

> Titus 2:13—"We wait for the blessed hope—the glorious appearing of our great God and Savior, Jesus Christ."

> Hebrews 6:19-20—"We have this hope as an anchor for the soul, firm and secure. It enters the inner sanctuary behind the curtain, where Jesus, who went before us, has entered on our behalf."

> 1 Peter 1:3—"God . . . has given us new birth into a living hope through the resurrection of Jesus Christ from the dead."

In each of those passages hope is a certain thing. For even though we do not possess the hoped-for thing yet, we are certain of it since it has been won for us by Christ and has been promised to us by God, "who does not lie." Clearly, those who have been justified are to look forward to their final and full glorification with confidence.

The *second* and last point is this. In 1 John 3:2-3 the apostle is speaking of the return of Jesus Christ and of the fact that when he appears, we shall be like him. He calls this our "hope." But this is not something having to do only with the future, says John. It has a present significance too. "Dear friends, now we are children of God, and what we will be has not yet been made known. But we know that when he appears, we shall be like him, for we shall see him as he is. *Everyone who has this hope in him purifies himself, just as he is pure.*" Our hope that we will be like Jesus motivates us to be like him now. It leads us to live as pure a life as possible.

Chapter 8

FALLING FROM GRACE

---

*You who are trying to be justified by law have been
alienated from Christ; you have fallen away
from grace. GALATIANS 5:4*

In the fifth chapter of Galatians there is a reference to grace that
has assumed an importance in some people's thinking far beyond
the apostle Paul's use of it and entirely out of keeping with his
context. It is the phrase *fallen from grace*. Perhaps it came to your
mind when I was writing about "standing in grace" in the last
chapter.

The point of the last chapter was that Christians have been given
a new standing before God because of grace. They have been
justified, and having been justified, nothing can remove them from
it. But if that is true, how can Paul speak about falling from grace
in Galatians? Doesn't that mean that a believer's salvation can be
lost? I grew up in an evangelical church where people thought that
way. They were afraid that they might lose their salvation. I remember a prayer meeting in which one of the women was crying about
the behavior of her daughter. The daughter was a Christian, but she

had been going to the movies, which this woman thought was sinful. "What if the Lord should return while my daughter is in a movie?" she asked. She believed that the daughter would not be taken to heaven. She would be lost. She was afraid that her daughter had "fallen from grace" and might perish.

The answer is that this is not what the phrase *fallen from grace* means. The words do not mean that if a Christian sins, he or she falls from grace and thereby loses salvation. There is a sense in which to fall into sin is to fall *into* grace, because God is gracious to us even when we sin. But to fall *from* grace is a different matter. To fall from grace is to fall into legalism, since to choose legalism is to abandon grace as the principle by which a person wants to be related to God. It is to turn away from the all-sufficient saving work of Jesus Christ.

This is what Galatians is about. Therefore, at this point in our study we need to look at Galatians and its teaching. In Galatians the word *grace* occurs eight times (in 1:3, 6, 15; 2:9, 21; 3:18; 5:4; and 6:18).

The Crisis in Galatia

Galatians is one of the most significant documents of religious history, second perhaps only to Paul's great letter to the Romans. Galatians was the cornerstone of the Protestant Reformation, Martin Luther having called it his Catherine von Bora because, as he said, "I am wedded to it." Galatians has been called the Magna Charta of Christian liberty. It was born in crisis, the first great crisis to face the emerging Christian church.

When the gospel first began to be preached in Judea, it was preached largely to Jews, and because the church was more or less homogeneous, its early internal development progressed smoothly. But Christianity is a worldwide religion, and as the gospel began to move outward from Jerusalem and churches that were largely Gentile began to be established, questions inevitably arose about a Gentile Christian's relationship to the law of Moses and to Judaism. Was the church to open her doors to all comers, regardless of their relationship to the law and Judaism? That is, could the church be Gentile without being Jewish first? Or was the church to be at heart merely an extension of Judaism to the Gentiles?

To put this in more specific terms, was it necessary for a Gentile believer in Christ to keep the law of Moses to be a Christian? Should he be circumcised? Should he or she observe the Jewish feasts and keep the dietary laws of Judaism, eating only kosher food?

Galatians is a record of the form this struggle took in the area of southern Asia Minor known as Galatia, but it is also a reflection of how the issue was being debated in Jerusalem and in Antioch in Syria.

Paul had visited Galatia on his first missionary journey, preaching and establishing churches in such cities as Iconium, Lystra, and Derbe (Acts 14). As usual, he had preached a gospel of God's grace. He taught that salvation is never to be sought by human works, even by strict attempts to obey the law of Moses. We are incapable of obedience and can never bring anything but God's righteous judgment on ourselves. Law can only condemn us. Therefore, if we are to be saved, salvation must come by a different means entirely. It must be provided by God through the work of his Son, the Lord Jesus Christ, and be received through faith.

The Galatians had received this gospel at the time. But some time after Paul's visit conservative Jewish teachers had arrived in Galatia from Jerusalem, claiming that Paul was mistaken in his teaching. They said that mere faith in Christ was not enough for salvation. Faith was good. But for those who wanted to be

Christians it was also necessary to come under the full authority of the Old Testament. Gentiles could have Jesus, but they had to have Moses, too. They could have grace, but they also needed to be circumcised. After all, God had given the law. Who was Paul, or anyone else, to disregard it?

Paul did not teach disregard for the law, of course. The book of Romans explains in considerable detail how the law is to function and why salvation by grace does not lead to antinomianism. We will come to that in time in these studies. But that was not the issue here. The Jerusalem legalizers—that is what they were called—were teaching that works, that is, obeying the law, were necessary for salvation. And that was an outright repudiation of the gospel, according to Paul's understanding. Paul was filled with indignation. He saw in a moment that if the views of the legalizers won out, grace and the Cross of Jesus Christ would be emptied of all value.

"Mark my words!" he said. "I, Paul, tell you that if you let yourselves be circumcised, Christ will be of no value to you at all. Again I declare to every man who lets himself be circumcised that he is obligated to obey the whole law. You who are trying to be justified by law have been alienated from Christ; you have fallen away from grace" (Gal. 5:2-4). His emphatic assertion means that if a person is trying to be saved by works, that person has fallen from grace into legalism and therefore cannot be saved, since no one can be saved by legalism.

Three Charges

As we read Paul's letter, we are aware that Paul was facing three devastating charges from his opponents: *first*, that he was no true apostle; *second*, that the gospel he preached was no true gospel; and *third*, that the gospel he did preach leads to loose living. Paul answered these charges in the three major sections of the letter: the first in chapters 1 and 2; the second in chapters 3 and 4; the third in chapters 5 and 6.

1. The charge that Paul was no true apostle.

Paul had been called to be an apostle by Jesus Christ, which means that he had received special revelation about the gospel from Jesus and had been given authority to preach it and to establish and govern Christian churches. But now his enemies were saying that he was not a true apostle. After all, he had not lived with Jesus when Jesus was on earth, as the "true" apostles had. He was not one of the Twelve. In truth, he was just an evangelist who, after he had received some small knowledge of Christianity, turned to his own devices and invented a gospel that would be pleasing to Gentiles in order to gain favor with them and advance his career.

Paul answers this charge by retelling the story of his life, especially the parts of it that involved his relationships to the other apostles.

First, he argues in the introduction (Gal. 1:6-10) that he had not been trying to please men, otherwise he would not have been preaching the gospel he had been preaching. The ones who were really trying to please their hearers rather than preach the true gospel were the legalizers. In what are some of the strongest words in the New Testament, Paul pronounces an anathema on these men: "Even if we or an angel from heaven should preach a gospel other than the one we preached to you, let him be eternally condemned!" And again, "If anybody is preaching to you a gospel other than what you accepted, let him be eternally condemned!" (vv. 8-9).

It is in reference to those harsh words that Paul then asks the Galatians, perhaps even with a bit of amusement, "Am I *now* trying to win the approval of men, or of God? Or am I trying to please men?" (v.10). People who are trying to please others do not go around pronouncing anathemas upon them.

Second, Paul admits that he did not get the gospel he had been preaching from the other apostles, but he turns the negative implication of that admission on its head, arguing that the very mark of an apostle is that he has *not* gotten his message from other men, but from God: "I want you to know, brothers, that the gospel I preached is not something that man made up. I did not receive it from any man, nor was I taught it; rather, I received it by revelation from Jesus Christ" (vv. 11-12). The next paragraph explains that after his conversion in Syria he did not go to Jerusalem, where he might be supposed to have learned the gospel from those who were apostles before him, but rather spent three years in Arabia. By the time he got to Jerusalem and met the others, his understanding of the gospel had already been well formed.

Third, on every occasion when he was in contact with the other apostles, which came later, he and his gospel were affirmed by them. That was true on his first visit to Jerusalem following his conversion, when he spent fifteen days with Peter (Gal. 1:18), and later at the Council of Jerusalem (Gal. 2:1-10, also described in Acts 15). As far as the Council of Jerusalem is concerned, Paul claims to have defended the gospel almost single-handedly for a time but to have been supported by the other apostles in the end. Equally important, the legalizers were repudiated. "James, Peter and John . . . gave me and Barnabas the right hand of fellowship when they recognized the grace given to me [and] agreed that we should go to the Gentiles" (Gal. 2:9).

Fourth, Paul provides an account of a disagreement he had with Peter when Peter came to Antioch. On that occasion Peter seemed to have wavered on the issue of Gentile liberty out of fear of what the legalistic Jews might think of him, separating himself from the Gentile Christians in order to eat only kosher food with the Jews. Paul calls this hypocrisy and tells how he rebuked Peter publicly: "You are a Jew, yet you live like a Gentile and not like a Jew. How is it, then, that you force Gentiles to follow Jewish customs?" (Gal. 2:14). The closing paragraphs of chapter 2 contain a summary of what he said to Peter and the others on that occasion, concluding, "I do not set aside the grace of God, for if righteousness could be gained through the law, Christ died for nothing!" (v. 21).

Paul shows how he stood for the truth of the gospel when Peter wavered, but he does not deny that Peter was a true apostle. In fact, it is Paul's significant achievement in the first portion of the letter that he asserts his own authority as an apostle without diminishing the true and legitimate authority of the others.

2. *The charge that Paul's gospel was no true gospel.*

The second charge against Paul followed from the first. If Paul was no true apostle, it was evident that the gospel he preached was no true gospel. On the other hand, if Paul was an apostle, then his gospel was the true gospel, and he had every right, indeed the duty, to expound it. This is what the next section of the letter does (chapters 3–4).

Paul's opponents had probably argued that because the law is God's law and is eternal in its effect (God's character does not change), keeping the law was and continues to be the way of salvation. They would have claimed that all who have ever been saved have kept the law. Jesus himself kept the law. So did his disciples. Who, then, was Paul to dismiss the requirements of the law as things unnecessary for salvation?

But that was not the issue. Those who are saved do keep the law. They are not lawbreakers. In fact, they keep the law in its true spirit, rather than in the letter only. Paul will make that point next, just as he does in Romans. The issue is not who does or who does not keep the law, but rather: What is the true basis upon which God reckons a sinful man or woman to be righteous?

Paul answers this charge and defends the true gospel in two ways.

First, he appeals to the Galatians' personal experience. When Paul went to Galatia he preached the gospel, the Galatians believed it, the Holy Spirit came upon them, and God even worked miracles in their midst. How did that happen? Paul asks. "I would like to learn just one thing from you: Did you receive the Spirit by observing the law, or by believing what you heard?" (Gal. 3:2). Obviously, it was by faith in Jesus and the gospel. Well, then, Paul continues, "Are you so foolish? After beginning with the Spirit, are you now trying to attain your goal by human effort?" (v. 3).

Presumably, the Galatians would acknowledge that God saved them through believing the gospel, not by observing the law, and that they ought therefore to continue their Christian life by faith and not by law, bowing to the legalizers' teaching.

Second, Paul argues his case from Scripture, primarily from the example of Abraham. Abraham was the father of the Jewish people, the greatest of the patriarchs. How was Abraham saved? As in Romans 4, Paul cites Genesis 15:6, where Scripture says: "[Abraham] believed God, and it was credited to him as righteousness" (Gal. 3:6). Abraham was not saved by law, since the law had not been given at that time. He was saved by believing God. Therefore, all who follow him are to be saved in precisely the same way. Paul observes that "the Scripture foresaw that God would justify the Gentiles by faith, and announced the gospel in advance to Abraham: 'All nations will be blessed through you.' So those who have faith are blessed along with Abraham, the man of faith" (vv. 8-9).

In this critical section of the letter Paul adopts an alternating argument, comparing the way of simple faith, on the one hand, with the way of law, on the other. The argument goes like this:

First point: *Abraham was saved by faith* (Gal. 3:6-9). Genesis 15:6, the first Old Testament text Paul cites, shows this to be true. The other Old Testament text, Genesis 12:3 (cf. 18:18; 22:18), shows that this must be true for everyone else, too, because it promises blessing for "all nations" and these have no physical descent from Abraham. The only way they can be part of the covenant of salvation is by faith.

Second point: *The law can only bring a curse* (Gal. 3:10-14). This is because we cannot keep it, and the law itself says, "Cursed is everyone who does not continue to do everything written in the Book of the Law" (Gal. 3:10; cf. Deut. 27:26). Jesus took our curse by his crucifixion.

Third point: *The covenant of salvation was established by God's promise to Abraham apart from works* (Gal. 3:15-18). The law had not even been given in Abraham's time; it came 430 years later.

Fourth point: *The law was given, not to save anyone, but rather to expose transgressions* (Gal. 3:19-25). The law is not a bad thing. The law would save us if we could keep it. Or rather, it would show that we do not need saving. We do, however. So when God gave the law 430 years after Abraham, it was to show that we are sinners and need salvation through faith in Jesus Christ. Paul says, "The law . . . was added because of transgressions until the Seed to whom the promise referred had come" (v. 19) and "The law was put in charge to lead us to Christ that we might be justified by faith" (v. 24). So the legalizers had a wrong starting point in their argument that: (1) God gave the law, (2) God does not change, and therefore (3) keeping the law continues to be the way of salvation. Their error was not understanding that God never gave the law as a way of salvation in the first place.

Fifth point: *Faith makes us sons of God and God's heirs* (Gal. 3:23-29). The law does not join us to Christ. Only faith does that, and it is only by belonging to Christ that we can become Abraham's seed and God's heirs.

Sixth point: *The law keeps us in the position of slaves* (Gal. 4:1-7). "But when the time had fully come, God sent his Son, born of a woman, born under law, to redeem those under law, that we might receive the full rights of sons" (vv. 4-5).

The last parts of this middle section (chapters 3–4) contain an impassioned appeal to the Galatians to continue on in faith (Gal. 4:8-20), followed by an allegory in which Sarah (Abraham's wife), Isaac, and Jerusalem stand for salvation by the grace of God through faith, and Hagar, Ishmael (Abraham's son by Hagar), and Mount Sinai stand for law-observance. The point is that those who are being saved are descended spiritually from Isaac and not from Ishmael, who was born of the slave woman.

3. The charge that the gospel Paul preached leads to loose living.

The charge was that Paul's gospel abolished restraints against sin. The Jews had the law, and they had stressed rigorous morality. Therefore, they looked down on Gentiles who did not have the law and lived immoral lives. What would happen if the law should be removed from Gentile churches? Clearly, lawlessness would increase and immorality would rise, according to the legalizers.

In the final section of the letter (chs. 5–6), Paul argues that this is not true. And the reason is that real Christianity does not lead a believer away from the law into nothing, still less into lawlessness. Rather it leads him to Jesus Christ. And that means, to put it in other language, that the Holy Spirit comes to live within the Christian, giving the person a new nature, creating love for God and a desire to obey him, and providing the ability to do what God requires. In other words, the gospel leads to an internal transformation. So it is from within, rather than from without, that the Holy Spirit produces good behavior. The key texts say:

> In Christ Jesus neither circumcision nor uncircumcision has any value. The only thing that counts is faith expressing itself through love. (Gal. 5:6)

> You, my brothers, were called to be free. But do not use your freedom to indulge the sinful nature; rather, serve one another in love. (Gal. 5:13)

> So I say, live by the Spirit, and you will not gratify the desires of the sinful nature. (Gal. 5:16)

> The fruit of the Spirit is love, joy, peace, patience, kindness, goodness, faithfulness, gentleness and self-control. Against such things there is no law. (Gal. 5:22-23)

According to these verses, life by the power of the Holy Spirit is entirely different from either legalism or lawlessness. Legalism imposes an outward code, but it does not change a person's inner nature to enable him or her to please God. Lawlessness gives vent to the sinful nature, allowing the unregenerate person to express himself in self-indulgence and debauchery. Christianity maintains the moral law but also provides the inner desire and power to obey God and so be all God intended us to be, which is true freedom, and to serve God fully.

Therefore Stand

The verse at the beginning of chapter 5 is at once both the high point and key to the entire letter: "It is for freedom that Christ has set us free. Stand firm, then, and do not let yourselves be burdened again by a yoke of slavery." The first part of the verse sums up the preceding four chapters. The second part is a challenge from which the ending of the letter flows. To put it in the terms of this study, Paul is saying, "Do not fall from grace. Rather, stand in grace."

Why? For the following reasons:

1. Legalism does not lead to holy living.

Normally we think it does because whenever something is not right or some great wrong is done, our natural instinct is to pass a law to correct it. And with the law goes punishment. If a person disobeys the law, he or she should be punished. Impose a fine. Send the criminal to jail. Execute the murderers. But even our own culture should tell us that this does not work. To some extent law does restrain evil actions. We might not do something for fear of getting caught. That is one reason God gave the law, to restrain sin. But neither law nor punishment produces holiness. And if the truth be told, law and the fear of punishment do not even restrain sin very much.

What is the problem? The problem is that sin is seated in the heart and passing laws is at best only an external attempt to solve the sin problem.

Jesus said this when he was explaining the dietary rules of his day. He said, "Nothing outside a man can make him 'unclean' by going into him. Rather, it is what comes out of a man that makes him 'unclean.' . . . For from within, out of men's hearts, come evil thoughts, sexual immorality, theft, murder, adultery, greed, malice, deceit, lewdness, envy, slander, arrogance and folly" (Mark 7:15, 21-22). This is why despotic political regimes never produce morality among their citizens but only feed corruption. I would argue that the only time any nation ever really moves forward in the area of morality is in periods of spiritual revival.

2. Legalism produces bondage.

Not only does legalism fail to produce what its defenders seek—that is, it does not produce morality—it actually has a contrary and harmful effect if it is seriously pursued. It produces bondage. Don't you know people who always seem to be trying to live their lives by rules? People who are constantly afraid that they might transgress some legal or moral boundary and be knocked down by God? They are not free people. They are not even happy. They are oppressed, sad, grim, burdened, and discouraged.

Paul says that to live this way is to be "burdened again by a yoke of slavery" (Gal. 5:1). The Jews of his day often referred to becoming a member of the covenant people of Israel as taking on "the yoke of the law." They considered it to be their glory. But it was a heavy yoke, and Paul calls it the yoke of a slave, just as a yoke placed on the neck of a farm animal was to harness the animal for hard work. This is what the apostle Peter was referring to at the Council of Jerusalem, recorded in Acts 15, when he advised against imposing the yoke of the law of Moses on the Gentiles. He said, "Why do you try to test God by putting on the necks of the disciples a yoke that neither we nor our fathers have been able to bear?" (Acts 15:10). According to Peter, this yoke was not only difficult to bear; it was impossible. According to Paul, it was slavery.

3. True holiness is the product of the Christian's new nature and is produced by his or her love for Jesus Christ.

It is why Paul says, "The only thing that counts is faith expressing itself through love" (Gal. 5:6). But let me illustrate that by a story.

Donald Gray Barnhouse was counseling a man who had met a fine Christian girl and wanted to marry her but was afraid to do so because of his sinful past. He was afraid to tell her of his past, and afraid that some of his old sinful habits might get the better of him and cause him to betray her love and hurt her deeply. Barnhouse counseled him to be open with the woman, telling her briefly about the nature of his past sins. "If you are going to be spending your lives together, there should be no barriers between you, and her knowledge of your weakness will help you all along the road," he said.

Then he told him about another couple he had heard of not long before. The point of the illustration is in what the young man said to him when he had finished. The man in this story had also lived a sinful life before his conversion, had met the Christian woman to whom he was now married, and had confessed the nature of his past to her. She was a spiritually mature woman, and she replied, "John, I want you to know that I have studied the Bible for a long time and am aware of what the human heart is like. I know we are all capable of terrible sin and that you might fall into it. I also know that if you do—I pray you will not—but if you do, the devil will tell you that you will never be able to live the Christian life, that you might as well give up and continue sinning, and that above all else you should never tell me because it will hurt me. But I tell you this now. This is your home. When I married you, I married your sinful nature as well as your regenerate nature, and I want you to know that there is full pardon and forgiveness in advance for any evil that may ever come into your life."

As he had been listening to this the man Barnhouse was counseling had bowed his head in his hands, obviously deeply moved. But when the end of the story came, he lifted his face, looked Barnhouse in the eyes, and said with great insight, reverently, "My God! If anything could ever keep a man straight, that would be it."

Suppose the woman in the second story had approached her husband's confession legalistically. Suppose she had said, "So that's what your life has been like! Well, I want you to know that if I ever get wind of any hanky-panky on your part, I'll really give it to you when you get home. See this rolling pin? I'll hit you over the head with it." If she had said that, the man might have mused, *So she wants to play that game, does she? Well, I'll just be careful then. I'll do what I want. I'll just be sure not to get caught.*

Legalism does not produce righteousness.

But love does. And it is by love that God has chosen to lead us onward in the Christian life. The Bible says, "God demonstrates his own love for us in this: While we were still sinners, Christ died for us" (Rom. 5:8).

God loves you and has been exceedingly gracious to you. He has proved it by sending Jesus Christ to die in your place. If you know that and really understand it, you will determine in your heart never to violate the wonder of such a great love. And the love you have for Jesus, as well as his love for you, will enable you to both stand in grace and grow in holiness.

Chapter 9

ABOUNDING GRACE

Where sin increased, grace increased all the more, so that, just as sin reigned in death, so also grace might reign through righteousness to bring eternal life through Jesus Christ our Lord. ROMANS 5:20-21

The last two verses of Romans 5 are among the truly great verses of the Bible. In the midst of a book in which every sentence is great, Romans 5:20-21 stands out like a brilliant beacon on a dark night. The dark background is sin and its horrible proliferation in the world. But the beacon flashes brightly.

This is the climax of a passage that contains a greater concentration of the word *grace* than any other similar passage in the Bible—five times in verses 15-21.

John Bunyan's Text

Romans 5:20 was a favorite text of John Bunyan, best known as the author of *Pilgrim's Progress*. That book reflects Bunyan's deep

THE GLORY OF GOD'S GRACE

spiritual experience, but the details of his life are spelled out best in his classic devotional autobiography, *Grace Abounding to the Chief of Sinners*. The title is taken from our passage, which said, in the King James Version that Bunyan used, "Where sin abounded, grace did much more abound," and from 1 Timothy 1:15, where Paul refers to himself as the "chief" of sinners (KJV).

Bunyan was born in 1628 of poor parents. His father was a traveling tinker, that is, a mender of pots and pans, and Bunyan practiced this trade for a time, so that he became known as "the tinker of Bedford." He had little education. In his youth he was profligate. In time he became troubled by an acute sense of sin. He wrote of himself that in those days it seemed as if the sun that was shining in the heavens begrudged him its light and as if the very stones in the street and the tiles on the houses had turned against him. He felt that he was abhorred by them and was not fit to live among them or benefit from them, because he had "sinned against the Savior."

God saved Bunyan and gave him great peace, and the title of his book is his testimony to what he discovered. He discovered that, no matter how great his sin was, the grace of God proved greater.

These verses are so wonderful that it is difficult to do justice to them in translation. In the New International Version the word *increase* is used three times in verse 20: twice of sin, which is said to have "increased," and once of grace, said to have "increased all the more." This is reasonably accurate, but it is weak, because in Greek Paul used two different words for the two kinds of increase, and the strength of the verse is enhanced by the resulting contrast.

The verb that refers to sin (*pleonatzō*) is based on the word *polus*, meaning "much" or "many." So it has the idea of a numerical increase. The NIV translation of this word is not bad. However, the second verb is quite different. It is *perisseuō*, which means "to abound," "overflow," or "have more than enough."

This verb does not have to do with numbers so much as with "excess." However, lest we miss the point, Paul adds the prefix *hyper* (we would say "super"), which gives the word the sense of "super excess" or "super abundance."

Most people probably know the text best in the King James Version, the version known to John Bunyan. It uses the idea of "abundance" for both parts of the comparison: "But where sin abounded, grace did much more abound." The New American and the Revised Standard Bibles do better by using *increase* for the first part and *abound* for the second: "Where sin increased, grace abounded all the more."

But how about this? The New English Bible says, "Where sin was thus multiplied, grace immeasurably exceeded it."

Or this? J. B. Phillips paraphrases the verse, saying, "Though sin is shown to be wide and deep, thank God his grace is wider and deeper still."

Even this does not seem to satisfy some commentators. Donald Grey Barnhouse suggested, "Where sin reached a high-water mark, grace completely flooded the world." D. Martin Lloyd-Jones used the word *engulfed*, calling grace a "flood" that sweeps everything before it.

What Paul says of grace in verse 20 prepares us for what he is going to say in the continuation of the sentence, for he is going to show that although sin has triumphed over us, doing great damage, grace has triumphed over sin and now reigns victoriously.

No Withholding of Grace

These verses say several important things about grace. First, *grace is not withheld because of sin*. We need to understand this clearly, because in normal life you and I do not operate this way.

If we are offended by somebody, we tend to withdraw from the person and withhold favor. If people offend us greatly, we find it hard even to be civil. God is not like this. On the contrary, where sin increases, grace superabounds.

What happened when Adam and Eve sinned? We saw the answer in the first chapters—they feared that grace would be withdrawn. God had been good to them. They had rebelled against his law concerning the forbidden tree, and God had said, "You must not eat from the tree of the knowledge of good and evil, for when you eat of it you will surely die" (Gen. 2:17). When God came to them, calling in the Garden, they hid in terror, thinking that the judgment God had threatened would now be executed. Instead, they found grace. God did not withhold grace because of Adam and Eve's sin. He made great promises of grace, announcing that the Messiah would come to destroy the work of Satan and bring the man and woman back to Paradise. Adam and Eve tried to cover their shame with fig leaves, but God clothed them with the skins of animals, which represented Christ's righteousness. Grace was not withheld from Adam and Eve; grace was given in spite of sin.

It was the same in the days of Moses, when the people had come to Mount Sinai and the law was being given. On the mountain God told Moses, "I am the LORD your God, who brought you out of Egypt, out of the land of slavery. You shall have no other gods before me" (Exod. 20:2-3). But while God was saying that, the people he had brought out of Egypt were breaking, not only this command, but also all the other commands he was giving. They were taking his name in vain, dishonoring their fathers and mothers, committing adultery, stealing, bearing false witness, coveting, and doing many other wicked things besides. Was this a barrier to God's grace? Not at all. On the very mountain from which he had looked down on the sin of this people, God gave specifications for the construction of the tabernacle with its altar and laws concerning the priesthood. He instituted ceremonies that showed the method by which sinful men and women could approach the holy God. Grace was not withheld from Israel because of sin. On the contrary, where sin increased, grace abounded all the more.

We come to the New Testament, and the principle unfolds with even greater splendor. The Son of God appeared on earth as the perfection of every grace. But instead of receiving him, his own people hounded him to death. Pilate would have released him, but the people, urged on by their corrupt spiritual leaders, shouted, "Crucify him! Crucify him!" So Pilate did. But even as he was being crucified, Jesus prayed for those who were causing his pain, saying, "Father, forgive them, for they do not know what they are doing" (Luke 23:34). And it was by his death that Jesus made atonement for our sins and opened heaven to those who should believe on him as their Savior. Even so great a sin as crucifying the Son of God did not cause grace to be withheld. Rather, where sin increased, grace abounded all the more.

What of the disciples? Peter had denied his Lord with oaths and cursings. But Jesus did not condemn Peter. Instead, Jesus appeared to him personally following the resurrection (1 Cor. 15:5) and later recommissioned him to service (John 21:15-22).

"Simon son of John, do you truly love me more than these?" asked Jesus.

"Yes, Lord, you know that I love you," Peter answered.

Then you must "feed my lambs," Jesus countered.

Paul experienced the same thing. Paul's testimony is nearly identical to Bunyan's, which is why Bunyan used Paul's words to depict his experience. Paul told the Corinthians,

> I am the least of the apostles and do not even deserve
> to be called an apostle, because I persecuted the
> church of God. But by the grace of God I am what I
> am, and his grace to me was not without effect. No, I

worked harder than all of them—yet not I, but the
grace of God that was with me. (1 Cor. 15:9-10)

Near the end of his life Paul wrote to his young coworker
Timothy:

Even though I was once a blasphemer and a persecutor and a violent man, I was shown mercy because I
acted in ignorance and unbelief. The grace of our
Lord was poured out on me abundantly [here he uses
a combination of the two words found in Romans
5:20, the first of the two verbs plus the emphasizing
prefix *hyper*, which is part of the second], along with
the faith and love that are in Christ Jesus. Here is a
trustworthy saying that deserves full acceptance:
Christ Jesus came into the world to save sinners—of
whom I am the worst. But for that very reason I was
shown mercy so that in me, the worst of sinners,
Christ Jesus might display his unlimited patience as
an example for those who would believe on him and
receive eternal life. (1 Tim. 1:13-16)

Now we come to you.

Today most people have very little awareness of their sin,
which shows how desperate their condition has become. But
perhaps you are one who, like John Bunyan, *is* aware of it. You
may consider yourself to have forfeited all hope of salvation by
some sinful action that rises up before you like a great concrete
dam against grace. I do not know what that sin is. It may be some
gross sexual sin or adultery.

It may be a perversion.

Perhaps you have stolen from your employer or your parents
or someone else who is close to you.

Could you have murdered somebody? Destroyed somebody's
life work or reputation?

Perhaps you remember a time in your life when you were so tyrannized by sin that you lashed out against God with blasphemies. Perhaps you cursed God. When you think back on those days—they may not be far in the past—you shudder and tremble. You are sure you have passed beyond all bounds of hope, that you are destined to be lost eternally.

If you are such a person—fortunate at least in your knowledge of your sinfulness—then this text is a proclamation of hope for you: "Where sin increased, grace increased all the more." Where sin multiplied, grace overflowed! No dam erected by sin can stop the abundant flow of God's grace. Grace is never withheld because of sin—not Adam's sin, not the sin of the people at Sinai, not Israel's sin, not Peter's sin, not Paul's sin, not John Bunyan's sin . . . not your sin. You may come to God through faith in Jesus Christ. Right now. Regardless of what you have done. In Jesus you can find full and immediate forgiveness.

No Reduction of Grace

The second thing these verses teach about God's superabounding grace is that it is *not proportioned according to sin.* There are two errors corrected here.

First, there are people who suppose that God is looking down on mankind and that he sees a great variety of people. One man is fairly good, but he is not perfect. He can only be saved by grace. So God dips into his bucket of grace and splashes out just enough for this man to find Christ and salvation. Here is another person, a woman. She is not so good. She needs more grace. Finally, here is a terrible person. He has committed every sin in the book, and he is not the least bit inclined toward God or godliness. By grace this man is also saved, but it takes a lot of grace to save him. God has to scrape the very bottom of the barrel to get this profligate in.

This is a gross misunderstanding. Grace is not something that makes up for our deficiencies. By grace God provides 100 percent of what is necessary for the salvation of 100 percent of the people he is saving. Grace is not measured out in proportion to our misdeeds.

Second, there are people who think like this: Here is a person who was once walking close to God but who fell into some great sin. I do not care what sin it is. It may have been Moses' sin, David's sin, your sin. But having fallen into sin, this person now thinks that he has forfeited something of God's grace. It is as if he had been given 100 percent of God's grace originally but supposes that now he is slowly wasting away this treasury of grace by his transgressions.

Do you ever find yourself thinking that? Are you thinking that now? That once you were a first-class Christian, but now, having sinned, you are condemned to be only a second-class or third-class Christian forever? Forget that. Your sin did not keep God's grace from flowing to you in full measure when you first came to Christ. It will not keep grace from you now.

I do not mean to suggest even for a moment that God condones sin. God hates sin so much that he sent Jesus Christ to die to rescue men and women from its destructive rule and tyranny. He hates sin in you. He will work to remove it and give you victory over it. In fact, if you do not grow in holiness and progressively triumph over sin, you are not regenerate. You are not a Christian. But the point I am making is that God will never diminish his grace toward you because of some sin. In fact—can I say it this way and not be misunderstood?—it is in your sin that you will most find grace to be abundant. The reason Paul was such a champion of grace was that he had been forgiven a great deal.

Grace Triumphant

The third point Romans 5:20-21 makes about grace is that *grace is powerful and triumphant.* Sin triumphed for a time, but although "sin reigned in death," grace is destined to "reign through righteousness to bring eternal life through Jesus Christ our Lord."

The illustration Paul uses is of two rival kingdoms, of grace and of sin. By personifying the power of sin, on the one hand, and the power of grace, on the other, he compares them to two kings. One king is a tyrant. He has invaded our world and has enforced a ruthless control over men and women. The end of this king's rule is death, for us and for all persons. This king's name is Sin. The other king is a gracious ruler. He has come to save us from sin and bring us into a realm of eternal happiness. The end of this king's rule is eternal life. His name is Grace.

The illustration tells us that grace is a power. We tend to think of grace as an attitude; and, of course, it is that. I have even defined it that way. I have called it "God's favor toward the undeserving," in fact, toward those who deserve the precise opposite. But more than an attitude, grace is also a power that reaches out to save those who, apart from the power of grace, would perish.

This means that grace is more than an offer of help. It is even more than help itself. To use the illustration of the two rival kingdoms, it would be possible to say that grace is an invasion by a good and legitimate king of territory that has been usurped by another. The battle is not always visible, because this is a matter of spiritual and not physical warfare. But the attack is every bit as massive and decisive as the invasion of the beaches of Normandy by the Allied forces at the turning point of the Second World War. The Allies threw their maximum combined weight into that great military encounter and won the day. Similarly, God has thrown his weight into grace, and grace will triumph.

All earthly kingdoms have a beginning: a military victory that brings a new monarch to the throne, a peaceful succession in which a new and able ruler takes over the helm of government and begins a new era of influence and prosperity, or an election of an outstanding ruler in a democratic land. So also with the kingdom of grace.

When was the kingdom of grace inaugurated?

The answer is "before the creation of the world" (1 Pet. 1:20). In that verse Peter is referring to the decision made in the eternal counsels of the Godhead in eternity past to send God's Son, the Lord Jesus Christ, to be our Redeemer. Theologians call this the Covenant of Redemption. It took place before the world was created.

In that eternal covenant between the persons of the Godhead, God the Father said, "I want to demonstrate the nature and power of my grace before the hosts of heaven. To do that I am going to create a world of creatures to be known as men and women. I am going to allow them to fall into sin. I am going to allow sin to reign over them, enslaving them by its power, and leading them at last to physical and spiritual death. But when sin has done its worst and the condition of the race seems most hopeless, I will send a heavenly being of infinite grace and power to rescue them and effect a new kingdom of love. Who will go for us? Who will accomplish the salvation of this yet-to-be-created race?"

The Lord Jesus Christ responded, "Here am I; send me. I will do what needs to be done. I will take the form of one of these creatures, thereby becoming man as well as God. I will die for them. I will bear the punishment of their transgressions. Then, when I have paid the penalty for their sin so that they will never have to suffer for it, I will rise from the dead and be for them an ever-reigning and ever-gracious Lord."

Earthly kingdoms also have a period of growth in which

territory is conquered and those who are to be part of the new kingdom are drawn into it. The kingdom of grace is the same. It also has grown and is growing. The stages have been something like this.

1. The announcement of the kingdom.

On the same day that Adam and Eve sinned, thus welcoming the contrary reign of sin and death into the world, God appeared in the Garden of Eden to foretell the coming of his Son. The words were spoken to Satan, who had caused Adam and Eve's fall.

> I will put enmity between you and the woman, and
> between your offspring and hers; he will crush
> your head, and you will strike his heel. (Gen. 3:15)

This was a prophecy of the incarnation of Jesus Christ and the Atonement, and although Adam and Eve did not understand it fully, they understood enough of it to believe God and look for the coming of the Redeemer. As a result, they became the first citizens of the kingdom.

2. Preparation for the kingdom.

The Old Testament records a period of preparation for the new king's coming. God established a godly line in the midst of the world's ungodliness, a line in which his name was remembered and faith in the coming Redeemer was kept alive. Seth, the third son of Adam and Eve, who replaced godly Abel after Cain had killed him, was the first of this new line. From Seth came the line of the godly antediluvians, including such persons as Enoch, who "walked with God," and Noah, who received grace at the time of the great Flood. Later Abraham was chosen, and from Abraham came Isaac, Jacob, and Jacob's sons, the twelve patriarchs of Israel. There were priests like Aaron, prophets like Isaiah and Jeremiah, and godly kings like David. On the eve of the birth of Jesus, there were people like Zechariah and Elizabeth, Joseph and Mary, Simeon and Anna, and others, all of whom looked forward to Christ's coming.

"These were all commended for their faith, yet none of them received what had been promised" (Heb. 11:39). They were saved by grace. They were part of the preparation for God's kingdom. But "the true light that gives light to every man was [only then] coming into the world" (John 1:9).

3. The launching of God's kingdom.

Since the death of the Lord Jesus Christ for sin is the launching of the kingdom we are not surprised to find Paul thinking of it as he unfolds his illustration. Grace reigns "through righteousness to bring eternal life through Jesus Christ our Lord."

His words remind us that grace does not mean setting aside God's law or the waiving of justice, as if God were merely to have said, "Well, you have been bad, but it does not matter; I forgive you." Sin does matter. It leads to death, death in this life and death in the age to come. God does not overlook sin. He deals with it. Christ died for it. Do you want to see the nature of God's kingdom? There is no place you will see it better than at Christ's cross. There grace and righteousness come together. Each is satisfied. It is by Jesus' death that eternal life is given to many.

4. Citizens of the kingdom.

It takes more than territory to make a kingdom. A kingdom requires subjects. Therefore, God is in the business of providing subjects for this kingdom. How? Theologians speak of it as the *ordo salutis* or the "order of salvation." It refers to the steps God takes to bring individuals into the kingdom of his Son. The Bible describes these steps as: foreknowledge, predestination or election, effectual calling, regeneration, repentance and faith, justification, sanctification, and, finally, glorification. No more glorious unfolding of the kingdom of grace toward individuals can be imagined. It is the power of God, providing for and then actually saving those who apart from it would certainly be lost. If grace were only a handout or an offer to help, we would perish. The only reason any of us are saved is because grace provides the way of salvation and then actually reaches out to turn us from sin and draw us to Christ.

Grace to a Slave of Slaves

In the first chapters we alluded to John Newton because of his well-known hymn "Amazing Grace," but I did not tell his story. Newton described himself in his autobiography as one who was, for a time, a "slave of slaves," and he was miraculously delivered by God. His deliverance is a great illustration of the power of God's abounding grace.

Newton lived from 1725 to 1807. He was raised in a Christian home in which he was taught verses of the Bible. But his mother died when he was only six years old, and he was sent to live with a relative who hated the Bible and mocked Christianity. One day, at an early age, Newton went to sea as an apprenticed seaman. He was wild and dissolute in those years, as John Bunyan had been. He had a reputation for being able to swear for two hours without repeating himself. At one point he was pressed into the British navy. But he deserted and was captured and then beaten publicly as a punishment. Eventually he was released into the merchant marine and went to Africa. Why Africa? In his memoirs he wrote that he went to Africa for one reason only and that was "that I might sin my fill."

In Africa Newton fell in with a Portuguese slave trader in whose home he was cruelly treated. This man often went away on slaving expeditions, and when he was gone his power passed to his African wife, the chief woman of his harem. She hated all white men and took out her hatred on Newton. He tells us that for months he was forced to grovel in the dirt, eating his food from the ground like a dog. He was beaten unmercifully if he touched it. In time, thin and emaciated, Newton made his way to the sea where he was picked up by a British ship making its way up the coast to England.

When the captain of the ship learned that the young man knew something about navigation as a result of being in the British navy, he made him a ship's mate. But even then Newton fell into trouble. One day, when the captain was ashore, Newton broke out the ship's supply of rum and got the crew drunk. He was so drunk himself that when the captain returned and struck him on the head, Newton fell overboard and would have drowned if one of the sailors had not hauled him back on deck just in time.

Near the end of a voyage, as they were approaching Scotland, the ship ran into bad weather and was blown off course. Water poured in, and it began to sink. The young profligate was sent down into the hold to pump water. The storm lasted for days. Newton was terrified. He was sure the ship would sink and he would drown. But there in the hold of the ship, as he pumped desperately for his life, the God of grace, whom he had tried to forget but who had never forgotten him, brought to his mind Bible verses he had learned in his home as a child. The way of salvation opened up to him. He was born again and transformed. Later, when the storm had passed and he was again in England, Newton began to study theology and eventually became a great preacher, first in a little town called Olney and later in London.

Of this storm William Cowper, the British poet who became

a personal friend of Newton and lived with him for several years, wrote:

> God moves in a mysterious way
> His wonders to perform;
> He plants his footsteps in the sea
> And rides upon the storm.

Newton was a great preacher of grace, for he had learned that where sin increased, grace abounded all the more. He is proof that the grace of God is sufficiently powerful to save anybody.

Chapter 10

LAW AND GRACE

What shall we say, then? Shall we go on sinning so that
grace may increase? By no means! We died to sin; how
can we live in it any longer? . . . Sin shall not be your
master, because you are not under law, but under grace.
ROMANS 6:1-2, 14

A number of years ago, when I was preaching through Romans
6 as part of a careful exposition of that book, I was in a Bible
college for some meetings and mentioned my upcoming series to
one of the Baptist professors. His reply was immediate: "Ah, that
is a good Baptist chapter for a Presbyterian." The comment took
me entirely off guard because the chapter has nothing to do with
baptism, as I understand it. In fact, the only reason I can think of
that this man might have said what he did is that Paul uses the
illustration of baptism in verses 3 and 4 to reinforce his earlier
point about our being united to Jesus Christ by God's grace.

Actually, the sixth chapter of Romans is a parenthesis dealing
with the first and most logical objection that anyone can bring
against the gospel: that it leads to lawless conduct.

What is the relationship of grace to law? Is it opposed to law? In one sense it is because, as we saw in our study of Galatians ("Falling from Grace," chapter 8), to fall from grace is to fall into legalism. A person who wants to be saved by law cannot be saved by grace, and vice versa. But does that mean that grace leads to license, to an utter disregard of God's law? It is here that Romans 6 comes in, for this important chapter teaches that grace does not lead to sinful conduct and, equally important, shows how righteous conduct actually comes about.

Not surprisingly, the answer is "by grace." The first half of the chapter (vv. 1-14) begins with grace: "Shall we go on sinning so that grace may increase?" (v. 1). It ends the same say: "For sin shall not be your master, because you are not under law, but under grace" (v. 14).

A Rational Objection

In the last study we were looking at the words "where sin increased, grace increased all the more" (Romans 5:20). We saw how wonderful they are. But they lead to the inevitable question Paul asks at the start of chapter 6: "Shall we go on sinning so that grace may increase?" If sin is overwhelmed by grace, why shouldn't we keep on sinning? Sin doesn't matter. Or, to make the objection even stronger, why not sin intentionally so that grace will increase proportionately and even more glory will be given to God?

The presence of this question is so reasonable that in one sense it is a test of whether or not a person's understanding of the gospel is sound. Most religious teaching is not. Most religions tell you that in order to get to heaven you must stop sinning and do good works, and, if you do this well enough and long enough, you will be saved. If a person is teaching along those lines, it is inconceivable that anyone would ever say to him, "Shall we go on sinning so that grace may increase?" A teacher like this is not talking about grace. He is talking about works, and his whole point is that salvation comes by doing them. To go on sinning is the exact opposite of his doctrine. No one ever raises that question to one who is teaching "works" righteousness.

But teach, as Paul did, that one is saved by grace apart from works, and the objection we are looking at is the first thing that comes to mind.

Yet the idea that God's grace should lead to sin is also irrational and unthinkable. Why is that? There are several reasons.

First, it overlooks God's *purpose* in the plan of salvation, which is to save us from sin. What does that mean? Does it mean to save us only from the punishment due us because of our sin? It does mean that, but not only that. We are justified by God in order that we might be saved from wrath at the final judgment, but that is only one part of God's plan. Well, then, does salvation mean that God is saving us from sin's guilt? Yes, that too. But again, not only that. Sin brings guilt, and one of the blessings of salvation is to be delivered from guilt, knowing that sin has been punished in Jesus Christ. Still deliverance from the guilt of sin is also only a part of what is involved. How about deliverance from sin's presence? Of course! But again, that only happens when we are glorified.

The important thing here is that God is also saving us from the practice of sin now. No one part of our deliverance from sin can rightly be separated from any other. So if we go on practicing sin now, we are contradicting the very purpose of God in our salvation.

Second, the antinomian objection is unthinkable because it overlooks God's *means* of saving sinners. Earlier we looked at the grace of God in our justification. Justification is the act by which God declares a person to be in a right standing before his justice due to the death of Jesus Christ. This is a wonderful truth, but it is not all that is involved. God justifies, but Jesus also redeems. God forgives, but the Holy Spirit also makes us spiritually alive so that we can perceive and embrace that wonderful forgiveness.

Indeed, what has Paul been talking about in Romans 5? He has been talking about the believer's union with Jesus Christ, hasn't he? And what is that union like? It is not a mechanical thing, still less a legal fiction. It is as vital as the union between a vine and its branches or between a head and the other parts of a person's body. If we are saved, we are "in Christ." If we are "in Christ," then he is in us and his life within us will turn us from sin to righteousness.

Dying to Sin

The reason grace does not lead to lawlessness is that those who have become Christians have "died to sin." This is the most important idea in Romans 6. It is introduced in verse 2, but it is repeated throughout the section, the words *died, dead,* or *death* occurring thirteen times. What does dying to sin mean? Let's begin by eliminating a few mistaken answers.

1. The Christian is no longer responsive to sin.

This is a very popular view, though a harmful one. It usually goes like this. What is it that most characterizes a dead body? It is that its senses cease to operate. It can no longer respond to stimuli. If you are walking along the street and see a dog lying by the curb, and you are uncertain whether or not it is alive, all you have to do to find out is nudge it with your foot. If it immediately jumps up and runs away, it is alive. If it only lies there, it is dead. In the same way, so this argument goes, the one who has died to sin is unresponsive to it. Sin does not touch such a person. When temptation comes, the believer neither feels nor responds to the temptation.

J. B. Phillips, the translator of one of the most popular New Testament paraphrases, seems to have held this view, because his rendering of Romans 6:7 reads, "a dead man can safely be said to be free from the power of sin" and of verse 11, that we are to look upon ourselves as "dead to the appeal and power of sin."

What should we say about this? The one thing in its favor is that it takes the tense of the Greek verb *died* at face value. It says that Christians have literally died to sin's appeal. But the problem with this interpretation is that it is patently untrue. There is no one like this, and anyone who is persuaded by this interpretation to think he is like this is due to be severely disillusioned. Moreover, it makes nonsense of Paul's appeal to Christians in verses 11-13. He says there, "Count yourselves dead to sin but alive to God in Christ. . . . Do not let sin reign in your mortal body. . . . Do not offer the parts of your body to sin, as instruments of wickedness." You do not urge a corpse to hold still. It will do that without your urging. We can dismiss this interpretation, even though it is held by many people.

2. The Christian should die to sin.

This view has been common in a certain type of holiness meeting, where the Christian is urged to die to sin. He is to "crucify the old man," which, he is told, is the secret to a "victorious" Christian life. The best thing that can be said for this view is that it is obviously correct to urge Christians not to sin. Indeed, that is what Paul himself will do later: "Do not let sin reign in your mortal body" (v. 12) and "Do not offer the parts of your body to sin" (v. 13). But aside from that, everything else about this view is in error. The starting point is wrong; it begins with man rather than with God. The image is wrong: one thing nobody can do is crucify himself. Above all the tense of the verb is wrong; for Paul is not saying that we ought to crucify ourselves (or die) but rather that we have died. He is telling us something that is already true if we are Christians.

3. The Christian is dying to sin day by day.

All this view means to say is that the one who is united to Christ will grow in holiness, and this is true. But it is not by increasingly dying to sin. It would be true to say that we will have to be as much on guard against sin's temptations at the very end of our life as we need to be now. To think of the verse as urging us to die to sin, though it touches on something true, nevertheless gets us away from the proper and only effective way of dealing with sin, which is to count on something that has already happened. This interpretation takes *died* as if it is an imperfect tense (*are dying*), rather than as an aorist (*have died*), which is what Paul actually says.

4. The Christian cannot continue in sin because he has renounced it.

This view carries no less weighty a name in its favor than that of Charles Hodge, a former great theology professor at Princeton Theological Seminary. Hodge noted the full aorist tense of the verb *died*, observing rightly that it refers to a specific act in our past history, and he sees that act as our renunciation of sin in order to follow Christ. This is a good interpretation for two reasons: (1) it recognizes the full force of the aorist verb *died*, and (2) what it says is true. Coming to Christ as Savior does involve a renunciation of sin; to renounce sin and to continue in it at the same time is a contradiction. If we had no other possible interpretations to go on, this would be an attractive explanation.

But there is a problem. In Hodge's interpretation "dying to sin" is something we do. It is our act, the act of accepting Christ. However, in Paul's development of the idea, "dying to sin" is not something we do or have done but rather something that has been done to us. It is the same as our being joined to Jesus Christ, which he is going to talk about in a moment under the figure of baptism. We did not join ourselves to Christ. Rather we were in Adam, and then God by his grace took us from that position and transferred us into the kingdom of his Son. It is because of that work that we are no longer to continue in sin, that doing so is unthinkable.

5. *The Christian has died to sin's guilt.*

This last mistaken understanding of the phrase *we died to sin* is Robert Haldane's. He sees it as having nothing to do with sanctification but rather with one result of justification, death to sin's guilt. What Haldane says is undoubtedly true as far as it goes. The justification of the believer has freed him or her from the guilt of sin, and it is true that in this sense the person has indeed died to it. As far as the guilt of sin and its resulting condemnation are concerned, sin no longer touches the Christian.

But that does not go far enough. True, we have died to sin's guilt. But what Paul is dealing with in this chapter is why we can no longer live in it. If all he is saying is that we are free from sin's condemnation, the question of verse 1 remains unanswered.

Our Old Life and Our New Life

It is obvious that, having rejected five important interpretations of the phrase *we died to sin*, including no less weighty interpretations than those of Charles Hodge and Robert Haldane, I must have a better view in mind—presumptuous as that may seem. But I think that is exactly what I do have, though I have certainly not invented it. It is expressed in various forms by such scholars as

F. Godet, John Murray, D. Martyn Lloyd-Jones, and John R. W. Stott.

In a short study titled *Men Made New* (Baker, 1984) Stott begins by noting that there are three verses in Romans 6 in which Paul uses the phrases *died [or dead] to sin:* verses 2, 10, and 11. In two of those instances, the first and the last, the reference is to Christian men and women. In the second of those verses the reference is to Christ. It is a sound principle of interpretation that whenever the same phrase occurs more than once in one context, it should be taken in the same way unless there are powerful reasons to the contrary. And if that is so, then the first question to ask in order to understand how we have died to sin is how Christ died to it. How did Jesus Christ die to sin?

The first answer we are inclined to give is that he died to sin by suffering its penalty. He was punished for our sin in our place. If we carry that through, we will come out near the position of Robert Haldane, thinking of justification only and of our death to sin's guilt.

But I want you to notice two things. First, the reference to Jesus' death in verse 10 does not say that he died *for* sin, though he did, but that he died *to* sin—the exact thing that is said of us. That seems to be a different idea. Second, Paul's statement does not say only that Christ "died to sin" but adds the very important words *once for all.* The full verse reads, "The death he died, he died to sin once for all; but the life he lives, he lives to God." This means that as far as sin is concerned, Jesus' relationship to it is finished. While he lived upon earth he had a certain relationship to it. He had come to die for sin, to put an end to its claims upon us. But now, having died, that phase of his life is past and will not be repeated. Verse 9, which leads into verse 10, says exactly that: "We know that since Christ was raised from the dead, he cannot die again; death no longer has mastery over him."

Now apply this understanding of "death to sin" to the other

two instances, which refer to us. How? By realizing that, as a result of our union with Christ in his death and resurrection, that old life of sin in Adam is past for us also. We can never go back to it. We have been brought from that old life, the end of which was death, into a new life, the end of which is righteousness. Therefore, since this is true of us, we must embrace the fact that it is true and live for righteousness.

Stott thinks of our biography being written in two volumes. Volume 1 is the story of the old man, of me before my conversion. Volume 2 is the story of the new man, of me after I have been made a new creation in Christ. Volume 1 of my biography ends with the judicial death of the old self. I was a sinner. I deserved to die, and I did die in the person of Jesus with whom I have become one. Volume 2 opens with my spiritual resurrection. I am now alive in him.

The First and Great Imperative

So what does that mean? What should I do in light of this teaching? Paul's answer is in verse 11: "In the same way, count yourselves dead to sin but alive to God in Christ Jesus."

This is an imperative. It is a command to do something. So let me begin by asking: How many times in Romans up to this point has Paul urged his readers to do something? That is, how many exhortations have there been? More than ten? Thirty? Less than five? The answer is that there have been none at all. This is the first time in five and a half chapters that the apostle has urged his readers to do anything.

What are they to do?

The verb is *count* (or *reckon*, as some of the other versions have it), in Greek, *logizomai*. It had two main uses:

1. *In commercial dealings.*

It was used in the sense of evaluating an object's worth or reckoning up a project's gains or losses. In other words, it was a bookkeeping term. We have preserved a bit of this in our English words *log*, *logistics*, and *logarithm*. A log is a numerical record of a ship or airplane's progress. *Logistics* is a military term dealing with the numbers and movement of troops or supplies. A logarithm is an exponent of a base number that equals another given number.

2. *In philosophy.*

It was used in the sense of sound, objective, or nonemotional reasoning. We have preserved this meaning in our English words *logic* and *logical*.

The common ground in these two uses of the word is that *logizomai* has to do with reality, that is, with things as they truly are. It has nothing to do with wishful thinking. Nor is it an activity that makes something come to pass or happen. It is an acknowledgment of or an acting upon something that is already true or has already happened. In bookkeeping, for example, it means posting in a ledger an amount corresponding to what exists. If I "reckon" in my passbook that I have $100, I must really have $100. If not, *reckoning* is the wrong word for me to be using. I am not reckoning. Deceiving myself (or others) would be more like it.

This has important bearing on what Paul is saying in Romans 6:11. For although he is proceeding in this chapter to the area of things we are to do and actions we are to take, his starting point is nevertheless our counting as true what God has himself already done for us.

This is so critical that I want to ask sharply: Do you really understand this? How can I say it clearly?

How about: The first step in our growth in holiness is counting as true what is in fact true.

How about: The way to a holy life is knowing that God has taken us out of Adam and has joined us to Jesus Christ, that we are no longer subject to the reign of sin and death but have been transferred to the kingdom of God's abounding grace.

How about: The secret to a holy life is believing God.

Paul says there are two things God has done that we are to count on. First, that we are *dead to sin*, if we are Christians. We have already seen how this is to be taken. It does not mean that we are immune to sin or temptation. It does not mean that we will not sin. It means that we are dead to the old life and cannot go back to it.

The second reality we are to count on is that we are now *alive to God in Christ Jesus*. This completes the parallel to verse 5, in which Paul said, "If we have been united with him like this in his death, we will certainly also be united with him in his resurrection." It explains how the earlier verse is to be taken. Our union with Jesus in his death is a present experience; we have died. So also is our union with him in his resurrection. Therefore, just as we have died to sin (and must count on it), so also have we been made alive to God in Jesus Christ (and must count on that also).

What does being made alive to God in Jesus Christ mean? Let me suggest a few of the changes that have taken place.

1. We have been reconciled to God.

In the earlier chapters of Romans there has been a grim sequence of terms: sin, wrath, judgment, death. But God has lifted us out of that downward-spiraling sequence by a set of opposing realities: grace, obedience, righteousness, eternal life. This means that we were subject to the wrath of God but that now, being in Christ, we are in a favored position before him. Before we were God's enemies. Now we are friends, and what is more important, he is a friend to us. There is a new relationship.

2. We have become new creatures in Christ.

Not only is there a new relationship between ourselves and God, which is wonderful in itself, but we have also become something we were not before. In 2 Corinthians Paul puts it like this: "If anyone is in Christ, he is a new creation; the old has gone, the new has come! All this is from God, who reconciled us to himself through Christ" (2 Cor. 5:17-18).

Another way of speaking about this is to speak of regeneration or of being born again, which was Jesus' term for it. He told Nicodemus, "You must be born again" (John 3:7). This was a deliberate backward reference to the way in which God breathed life into our first parent, Adam, so that he became "a living being" (Gen. 2:7). Before that, Adam was inert, a lifeless form. But when God breathed some of his breath into him, Adam became alive to God and all things. Likewise, God breathes new spiritual life into us by the work known as regeneration. We become something we were not before. We have new life, and that life is responsive to the one who gave it.

Before this, the Bible meant nothing to us when we read it or it was read in our hearing. Now the Bible is intensely alive and interesting to us. We hear the voice of God in it.

Before this, we had no interest in God's people. Christians acted in ways that were foreign to us. Their priorities were different from our own. Now they are our very best friends and coworkers. We love their company and cannot seem to get enough of it.

Before this, coming to church was boring. Now we are alive to God's presence in the service. Our worship times are the very best of our week.

Before this, service to others and witnessing to the lost seemed strange and senseless, even repulsive. Now they are a chief delight.

3. We are freed from sin's bondage.

Before we died to sin and were made alive to God, we were slaves of our sinful natures. Sin was ruining us. But even when we could see that clearly and acknowledge it, which was not often, we were still unable to do anything about it. We said, "I've got to stop drinking; it's killing me." Or, "I am going to ruin my reputation if I don't stop these sexual indulgences." Or, "I've got to get control of my temper," or "curb my spending," or whatever. But we were unable to do it. And even if we did get control of some important area of our life, perhaps with the help of a good therapist or friends or a supportive family, the general downward drift was unchanged. We really were *non posse non peccare* ("not able not to sin"), as Saint Augustine described it.

Being made alive to God, we discover that we are now freed from that destructive bondage. We still sin, but not always and not as often. And we know that we do not have to. We are now *posse non peccare* ("able not to sin"). We can achieve a real victory.

4. We are pressing forward to a sure destiny and new goals.

Before we were not. We were trapped by the world and by its time-bound, evil horizons. Being saved, we know that we are now destined for an eternity of fellowship and bliss with God. We have not reached it yet. We are not perfect. But we echo within what Paul said, describing his new life in Christ to the Philippians:

> Not that I have already obtained all this, or have already been made perfect, but I press on to take hold of that for which Christ Jesus took hold of me. Brothers, I do not consider myself yet to have taken hold of it. But one thing I do: Forgetting what is behind and straining toward what is ahead,

I press on toward the goal to win the prize for
which God has called me heavenward in Christ
Jesus. (Phil. 3:12-14)

5. We can no longer be satisfied with this world's weak offerings.

To be sure, the world never did really satisfy us. The world, which is finite, can never adequately fill beings who are made with an infinite capacity for fellowship with and enjoyment of God. But we *thought* the world and its values were satisfying. We expected to be filled.

Now we know that it will never work and that all we see about us, though it sometimes has value in a limited, earthly sense, is nevertheless passing away and will one day be completely forgotten. Our houses will be gone; our televisions will be gone; our beautiful furniture and cars and bank accounts (even our IRAs and Keoghs) will have passed away. So these tangible things no longer have any real hold on us. We have died to them, and in their place we have been made alive to God, who is intangible, invisible, and eternal, and of greater reality and substance than anything else we can imagine.

Therefore, we know ourselves to be only pilgrims here. We are passing through. Like Abraham, we are "looking forward to the city with foundations, whose architect and builder is God" (Heb. 11:10).

Nowhere to Go But Forward

Where do we go from here? Do we continue in a life of sin so that, as we might piously choose to put it, grace may increase? Or do we choose the other path, the path of Godlike conduct? By now we should be able to see that there is no true alternative.

The life of sin is what we have died to. There is no going back for us, any more than Jesus could go back to suffer and die for sin again. But if there is no going back—if that possibility has been eliminated—there is no direction for us to go but forward.

Some people try to find the key in an intense emotional experience, thinking that if only they can make themselves feel close to God, they will become holy. Others try to find sanctification through a special formula or methodology. They think that if they do certain things or follow a certain prescribed ritual, they will become holy. But godliness does not come in that way, and, in fact, approaches like these are deceiving. A holy life comes from *knowing*—I stress that word—*knowing* that you can't go back, that you have died to sin and been made alive to God. You are no more able to go back to your old life than an adult to his childhood.

Can an adult become a child or infant again? I suppose if he really wants to, he can act childish. But he can't actually become a child again. No more can a true Christian become a non-Christian, and that is the reason grace does not lead to lawless conduct. We cannot go back to sin or even continue in it. There is no way to go but forward.

Part Three

LIVING by GRACE

Chapter 11

STRONG IN GRACE

You then, my son, be strong in the grace that is in Christ Jesus. And the things you have heard me say in the presence of many witnesses entrust to reliable men who will also be qualified to teach others. 2 TIMOTHY 2:1-2

Several chapters ago I defined grace as "God's unmerited favor," and later we defined grace as "God's favor to those who actually deserve the opposite." There was nothing remarkable in those definitions. Thousands of Bible teachers have said the same thing, even in those identical words. But in this new section, it is important to expand that initial definition.

It is important because the Bible also expands it in the sense that it uses the word *grace* not only to describe the unmerited favor of God in salvation but also to describe the provision God makes to live a victorious Christian life. This is unmerited too. That is why it is called grace. But it is nevertheless a new thing. Nearly all the verses we are going to focus on in this third section of the book use the word in this way.

An example is 2 Corinthians 12:9, the verse we will be looking at in the next chapter: "My grace is sufficient for you, for my power is made perfect in weakness." Clearly, that verse is not talking about the grace of God in sending Jesus Christ to be our Savior, which is what we think of almost always when we hear the word *grace*. Rather it is speaking of the provision of help or strength to carry on in God's service in spite of some severe physical handicap or limitation. Hebrews 4:16 is another example: "Let us then approach the throne of grace with confidence, so that we may receive mercy and find grace to help us in our time of need." In this verse grace is actually explained as God's provision of "help . . . in our time of need."

We also need grace in this sense. We need it desperately, because without God's gracious daily provision of help we will never be able to live the Christian life, not even for a moment.

An Introduction to 2 Timothy

In 2 Timothy chapter 2, the old imprisoned apostle Paul gave his young protégé Timothy the charge: "You then, my son, be strong in the grace that is in Christ Jesus. And the things you have heard me say in the presence of many witnesses entrust to reliable men who will also be qualified to teach others" (vv. 1-2). It is necessary to understand a little about the epistle.

1. Second Timothy is the last of Paul's surviving letters.

Paul may have written many letters of which we have no record. But of the thirteen letters we do have, those that have been included in the New Testament canon (Romans, 1 and 2 Corinthians, Galatians, Ephesians, Philippians, Colossians, 1 and 2 Thessalonians, 1 and 2 Timothy, Titus, and Philemon), 2 Timothy was Paul's last. It was written from prison in Rome where Paul was awaiting martyrdom. In the last chapter he tells how his former friends have deserted him (v. 16), and he asks Timothy, the recipient of the letter, to come to him before winter, bringing a warm coat that he had left behind at Troas, plus some scrolls and parchments.

2. Timothy was a young man in an extremely demanding position.

He seems to have been led to Christ by Paul. That is why Paul calls him "my son" (2 Tim. 1:2; 2:1) and "my true son in the faith" (1 Tim. 1:2). He had traveled with Paul, and when Paul had left Ephesus for Macedonia, Timothy had been left in charge of the Asian churches (1 Tim. 1:3), just as Titus had been left in charge of the churches on Crete (Tit. 1:5).

But there were problems. Some of the problems were external. The leaders in Asia Minor had turned against Paul. Paul reports in the first chapter that "everyone in the province of Asia has deserted me, including Phygelus and Hermogenes" (2 Tim. 1:15). They were ridiculing Paul to the point where Timothy was tempted actually to be ashamed of him (1 Tim. 1:8). Also the churches themselves were corrupt. The third chapter describes these terrible conditions. To manage a fellowship of churches like that under those circumstances and in the absence of Paul and the position of strength he represented would have been an overwhelming challenge for nearly anybody. It certainly was for Timothy.

In addition, there were personal problems that involved Timothy himself. First, he was comparatively young (1 Tim. 4:12). By this time Paul had been in the ministry thirty or thirty-five years, he was an apostle, and even he was no longer given proper respect. How much less respect would his young protégé receive! Second, Timothy was prone to illness (1 Tim. 5:23), as a result of which he could not have made a strong impression or been an imposing presence. Finally, he must have been rather reserved—some would say timid—by temperament. This was not necessarily bad. If we had known Timothy, we would say that he had the gentle disposition and consistent thoughtfulness necessary to be a kind and encouraging pastor. But Timothy was no Paul! He possessed neither Paul's drive nor Paul's stamina, and yet he had been placed in a position in which he was to guard the gospel and guide the churches of Asia in these spiritually barren times.

3. Paul was concerned for the preservation of the gospel.

This note is a recurring theme throughout the letter, and in the first letter, too. "Timothy, guard what has been entrusted to your care," says Paul at the end of the first letter (1 Tim. 6:20). In the second letter he tells him: "Guard the good deposit that was entrusted to you—guard it with the help of the Holy Spirit who lives in us" (2 Tim. 1:14); "continue in what you have learned and have become convinced of, because you know those from whom you learned it" (2 Tim. 3:14); and "I give you this charge: Preach the Word; be prepared in season and out of season; correct, rebuke and encourage—with great patience and careful instruction" (2 Tim. 4:1-2). Paul earlier had written: "You then, my son, be strong in the grace that is in Christ Jesus. And the things you have heard me say in the presence of many witnesses entrust to reliable men who will also be qualified to teach others" (2 Tim. 2:1-2).

Paul had preserved the wholeness and purity of the gospel in his lifetime. He was about to be martyred. So he commits his charge to Timothy, who is instructed to guard the gospel, too.

As I read that charge, I find it extending over four generations: (1) God had entrusted the gospel to Paul, who (2) had entrusted the gospel to Timothy, who (3) was to entrust the gospel to faithful men, who (4) would be able to entrust it to others. That is the way the gospel must be passed on. It is the true apostolic succession. But Paul was afraid it would not happen in

Asia, and his concern that it might not is the burden of his letter to young Timothy.

What was Paul afraid of?

Let's be very blunt about it. He was afraid that Timothy might quit, the combination of the enormous challenge he faced and his own weak nature proving too much for him. I do not think he ever feared that Timothy would repudiate the gospel itself, as the other leaders in Asia had. Timothy was too well grounded for that. But he might give up. After all, no one had stood with Paul at his first trial (2 Tim. 4:16). Demas, his other coworker and friend, had deserted him and gone to Thessalonica (2 Tim. 4:10). Perhaps Timothy would desert the gospel, too. How would Paul provide for the Asian churches then? Who could he turn to if Timothy should drop out?

It is against this background that we must read our text. "You then, my son, be strong in the grace that is in Christ Jesus. And the things you have heard me say in the presence of many witnesses entrust to reliable men who will also be qualified to teach others" (2 Tim. 2:1-2). It means: Don't quit, Timothy. Keep on until others are prepared to hand the gospel on to their successors just as you have been faithful in handing it to them.

Don't you ever feel like quitting? Quitting the work God has given you? It may be Christian work, but I would not restrict the temptation to that. You may want to opt out of your marriage or some other relationship. You may want to quit a demanding or boring job. It could be anything.

You are not going to profit from 2 Timothy unless you recognize that the temptation Timothy had to quit is also your temptation, since you are no different from him. This is the problem with so much of what is said about Timothy being a weak, timorous person. He may have been. But if he was, he was no different from us, at least at the point where we are pressured to abandon our stand for Jesus Christ. When we call him weak, we are thinking of ourselves as being strong. But are we? Are you strong enough not to abandon the gospel or anything else God has given you to do in this life?

The letter mentions several pressure points that were affecting Timothy that could cause him to quit. As we look at them, we must ask ourselves if they are affecting us.

Pressure Point Number 1: Ridicule

The first of these three pressure points was ridicule. Paul discusses it in 2 Timothy 1, where he urges Timothy not to be ashamed of either the Lord, the gospel, or himself.

What a powerful weapon of Satan shame is! A disciple of Jesus Christ may be strong in many ways, able perhaps to stand against the worse kinds of physical threats. We may tell Jesus, as Peter did, "Even if I have to die with you, I will never disown you" (Mark 14:31). But if even a little servant girl makes fun of us, saying, "You also were with that Nazarene," a moment or two later we can be found denying we ever knew Jesus or professed the gospel. Peter said, "I don't know or understand what you're talking about" (Mark 14:67-68). In Asia everyone else had deserted Paul. It would have been easy for Timothy to go with the flow and so dissociate himself from Paul and the gospel he had fully and fearlessly taught.

Notice that the word *ashamed* occurs three times in chapter 1, in verses 8, 12, and 16. In verse 12, Paul says that he was not ashamed: "I am not ashamed, because I know whom I have believed, and am convinced that he is able to guard what I have entrusted to him for that day."

In verse 16, he refers to a man whose name was Onesiphorus, saying that he was not ashamed of Paul: "Onesiphorus . . . was not ashamed of my chains." When Onesiphorus got to Rome,

Paul was in prison. Apparently nearly everyone in the Roman church had forgotten Paul, because Onesiphorus had to search hard until he found him. But he did search, and when he found him he was not ashamed of him but rather stood by him and often refreshed him. This must have meant a great deal to Paul in such circumstances. It is why he commends Onesiphorus so forcefully and prays for him.

The remaining use of the word *ashamed* is in verse 8, and it refers to Timothy. Paul was not ashamed of the gospel. Onesiphorus was not ashamed of Paul. Timothy should not be ashamed either: "So do not be ashamed to testify about our Lord, or ashamed of me his prisoner. But join with me in suffering for the gospel, by the power of God, who has saved us and called us to a holy life" (vv. 8-9). This was no small matter. If Timothy had never been tempted to be ashamed of Paul, Paul would not have uttered this warning. If Paul had never been tempted to shame, he would not have insisted on his own personal stand against shame as strongly as he did (also in Rom. 1:16). Instead of being ashamed, Timothy should be willing to suffer for Jesus and the gospel. How can Timothy do this? How can we stand when all about us are going another way and making fun of us for our position? The answer is that God will help us. This is the main point of the letter. In chapter one it is expressed in verse 14: "Guard the good deposit that was entrusted to you—guard it *with the help of the Holy Spirit* who lives in us."

Pressure Point Number 2: Hardships

The second pressure point that might have moved Timothy to abandon his fight for the gospel was hardship, the theme of chapter 2. In the first chapter Timothy was encouraged to suffer for the gospel rather than being ashamed of it. In this chapter, one aspect of that suffering is spelled out, not that of ridicule or persecution, but rather of pure physical hardship. It is a recognition that standing for Jesus Christ in a world that is opposed to him and hates him is hard work.

In this chapter there are six metaphors to show what Timothy must be willing to be and do, rather than abandon his calling.

1. A soldier (vv. 3-4).

The Christian's life is a warfare, and it is not only against earthly enemies like those who may have been ridiculing Paul and Timothy but also "spiritual forces of evil in the heavenly realms" (Eph. 6:12). This is an unrelenting battle to the death. What kind of a soldier is needed for it? Obviously one who is trained for combat, obedient to orders, and hardened by rigorous military discipline. Verse 3 mentions hardships especially. In verse 4 Paul says that the good soldier will avoid "civilian affairs" or, as we might say, nonmilitary entanglements.

2. An athlete (v. 5).

An athlete does not put himself in harm's way, as a soldier does. But his course is no less rigorous and demanding. He exerts himself thoroughly in training, and in the contest he presses to the limits of his ability and strength to win a victory. Paul describes himself in these terms in 1 Corinthians, saying that he beat his body and even made it his slave so that he might attain the victor's prize (1 Cor. 9:24-27). In 2 Timothy his emphasis is on competing by the rules (v. 5).

3. A farmer (v. 6).

Two things immediately come to mind with this image. First, farming is hard physical work. It takes strenuous effort to prepare a field for planting—to plant, care for, and then harvest a crop, often in bad weather. Second, there is a lot of time between the work of sowing and the joy of harvesting. So a farmer must be patient. On the other hand, if he is hardworking and patient, the farmer will reap a harvest. Paul seems to have this in mind here, for he speaks of the farmer receiving "a share of the crops" and interrupts the flow of these metaphors to bring in the example of Jesus who died but who also rose again, assuring us that "if we endure, we will also reign with him" (v. 12).

4. A workman (v. 15).

A good workman knows his materials and can cut, fashion, or mold them to make the object he wants. In Timothy's case, the material to be used is the Word of God, the Bible, and the work is to teach it clearly. The Greek text of verse 15 ("to cut straight") means a bit more than any of the translations seems to convey, since the true meaning is probably to be measured against the errors of Hymenaeus and Philetus, whom Paul mentions. They had "wandered away from the truth" (v. 18). That is, their teaching was off the straight track. It was faulty. Consequently, anyone who followed it would go astray and miss the right destination. The Bible teacher who is "approved" by God does not deviate from the straight path of Bible teaching and therefore does not lead his listeners astray.

But that takes hard work. To begin with, the teacher has to understand the Bible itself, and that is not easy, since God's ways are not our ways nor are his thoughts our thoughts. To become a "Bible man or woman" means to have our whole way of thinking reordered. Second, the teacher needs to concentrate on things that are central rather than peripheral. This requires judgment honed by long hours in the Word. Third, he must work to develop true godliness in his listeners, and for that he must himself be godly. Finally, the teacher must seek approval of God and not that of other human beings. To seek human approval is a very great danger.

5. A household vessel (vv. 20-21).

The image of a workman or artisan probably suggested Paul's description of a Christian worker as a vessel used in a large house, since workmen make vessels, and a vessel alone of these metaphors is an impersonal object rather than a profession. Yet the image adds something new. It enables Paul to distinguish between impure vessels and those that have been cleansed for "noble purposes" and "good work" (v. 21). He means that the worker must possess personal godliness or holiness.

6. A servant (vv. 24-26).

The idea of a clean or pure vessel carries over into the last of Paul's six images, for he speaks of the worker being a servant in verses 24-26, and his emphasis here is on the servant's gentle, godly, and helpful character. Paul might have emphasized the hard work a slave was called upon to do, but he has already emphasized that sufficiently in the earlier metaphors. Here he is saying that the good servant must be like his good master. That is, we must be like Jesus Christ.

So how are we to be like this? And how are we to be able to endure the kind of hardness this chapter describes? In this case the answer is at the beginning of the chapter in the verse that mentions grace. It is by the help the God of grace supplies (v. 1). It is only in the Lord's strength and protected by his armor that we can fight these spiritual battles and be victorious (cf. Eph. 6:10-20).

Pressure Point Number 3: Sin in the Church

The third chapter of 2 Timothy is the chapter best known to most of us because of its description of the Bible as "God-breathed" and as being "useful for teaching, rebuking, correcting and training in righteousness, so that the man of God may be thoroughly equipped for every good work." The Bible is useful because it is "God-breathed." That is, it is unlike any other book. That is worth saying. B. B. Warfield argued it well many years ago.

But this is not all 2 Timothy 3 speaks to, and, in fact, it may not even be the most essential thing, since Timothy was certainly not questioning the Bible's character or truthfulness. He knew the Bible was the Word of God, just as we do. That was not his problem. The problem was: Is the Bible able to meet the needs of the hour when "evil men and impostors . . . go from bad to worse, deceiving and being deceived" (v. 13)? Will it suffice? Will the ministry Timothy was given as a teacher of the Bible prove effective in the long run so that he can continue in it and not quit? Or do we need something else, something more relevant or attractive or more powerful? Should Timothy abandon his position to those who are more attractive or entertaining?

Let's begin by noting that the days about which the apostle was warning Timothy are our days, or are at least indistinguishable from them.

Paul calls them "the last days" (2 Tim. 3:1). That can mean either of two things. It can mean the very last days, those immediately before the return of Jesus Christ. Or it can mean the period of time that will elapse between his first and second comings. I could argue for either. But I am most concerned to see that the characteristics of these days, wherever in time they are to be located, aptly describe the days in which I live.

We do not call the characteristics of our time by these words, of course. We rename our vices, as sinners regularly do.

Lovers of themselves? We call that the "new narcissism." We have even made it a virtue to which we cater in our mass advertising appeals. "I know it's expensive, but I'm worth it."

There is nothing nice or attractive about this vice. It is self-love, the root of all sin.

Lovers of money? The biblical word is *greed*, but we call it simply "materialism." Our economic system is based upon it. In our system men and women sell their souls and perish forever for the sake of material goods that do not even last for a lifetime.

Boastful, proud, abusive? We call this "self-esteem," but there is nothing worth esteeming in these terms. The first one actually refers to braggarts, the second to haughty people, the third to blasphemers. These persons think so highly of themselves that they look down on all others and despise God particularly.

Disobedient to parents? We call this the "generation gap" and so make light of it. But the Bible has harsh words for children who fail to respect their parents, as well as for all who reject authority.

So it continues. It is hard to think of a more apt or comprehensive description of the times in which we live, unless it is the more devastating catalogue of vices found in the latter half of Romans 1.

But there is something about this that is even more frightening than the vices Paul has listed, and that is what he says in 2 Timothy 3:2-4. For having described this evil future culture by the words *ungrateful, unholy, without love, unforgiving, slanderous, without self-control, brutal, not lovers of the good, treacherous, rash, conceited,* and *lovers of pleasure rather than lovers of God,* Paul adds what is surely the most shocking of all these statements, namely, "having a form of godliness but denying its power."

What does that mean? A "form of godliness" must refer to those who are pretending to be godly, and since this cannot describe pagans, it must describe those who are within the church. In other words, the problem is not that the world will be like what Paul is describing but that the church will be. It is that the church will be indistinguishable from the world and be equally corrupt, at least when you look beneath the surface.

What a problem! No wonder Jesus asked his disciples, "When the Son of Man comes, will he find faith on the earth?" (Luke 18:8).

What is young Timothy to do when he is faced with such a tremendous problem? Is he to look around for some new strategy? Is Paul going to reach down into his bag of ministerial tricks and come up with a new and secret weapon to fight this end-time apostasy and calamity? It is significant that Paul does nothing of the sort. Instead of something new, he tells Timothy to keep on with what he has. The Bible is all he needs because the Bible is from God. It is "God-breathed." Therefore it contains within it the power of God, and it accomplishes the will of God. Timothy is to be assured of this, and because he is assured of it, he is to continue to teach the Bible faithfully and with confidence. He is not to quit.

> But as for you, continue in what you have learned
> and have become convinced of, because you know
> those from whom you learned it, and how from in-
> fancy you have known the holy Scriptures, which
> are able to make you wise for salvation through
> faith in Christ Jesus. (2 Tim. 3:14-15)

It is another way of saying what we have read several times earlier. Paul means, "Be strong in the grace that is in Christ Jesus."

Stand Firm Then

The last chapter brings the entire letter to a moving climax. In this chapter Paul does not describe another "pressure point" but rather gives Timothy a final, solemn charge.

> In the presence of God and of Christ Jesus, who
> will judge the living and the dead, and in view of

his appearing and his kingdom, I give you this
charge: Preach the Word; be prepared in season
and out of season; correct, rebuke and encourage—
with great patience and careful instruction. For the
time will come when men will not put up with
sound doctrine. Instead, to suit their own desires,
they will gather around them a great number of
teachers to say what their itching ears want to hear.
They will turn their ears away from the truth and
turn aside to myths. But you, keep your head in all
situations, endure hardship, do the work of an evangelist, discharge all the duties of your ministry.
(2 Tim. 4:1-5)

What a tremendous charge, especially in light of the situation
in the church and world that Paul has described earlier! How
could Timothy possibly hope to carry it out?

As I read this, it seems to me that there are three answers.

First, this is God's charge to Timothy and the charge of the
Lord Jesus Christ, not merely Paul's charge. It is why Paul begins
as he does, saying, "In the presence of God and of Christ Jesus,
who will judge the living and the dead, and in view of his
appearing and his kingdom." The work may be hard, but it is
God who has given it to us. We cannot take his commissioning
lightly. We must be faithful to the end.

Second, others have done it. Paul had an even more difficult
time of ministry than Timothy, but Paul had come through,
having "fought the good fight," "finished the race" and "kept the
faith." When we are tempted to quit, let's remember that "no
temptation has seized you except what is common to man"—
even the temptation to quit—and that "God is faithful; he will
not let [us] be tempted beyond what [we] can bear" (1 Cor.
10:13).

And there is this too: "he will also provide a way out so that [we] can stand up under it," which leads us to the next point.

Third, God will provide the grace we need to be faithful. This is what the end of 2 Timothy says. It looks like mere personal notes, as in most of Paul's letters. But it is far more. It describes the situation Paul is in. Demas has deserted him. Everyone but Luke has departed. Alexander the metalworker did him great harm. At his first trial, no one came to his support. But the God of grace was with him. "The Lord stood at my side and gave me strength, so that through me the message might be fully proclaimed and all the Gentiles might hear it. And I was delivered from the lion's mouth" (v. 17).

There it is! If you determine to stand for God without quitting, you find that God will stand with you. He will rescue you from every evil attack and in the end bring you "safely to his heavenly kingdom" (v. 18).

Chapter 12

MY GRACE IS
SUFFICIENT FOR YOU

---

*My grace is sufficient for you, for my power is made
perfect in weakness. 2 CORINTHIANS 12:9*

In the last chapter we looked at 2 Corinthians 12:9 as a verse in
which grace refers to God's helping us to live a strong Christian
life. That verse goes a step beyond merely standing for God
against such things as ridicule, hardship, and corruption in the
church. Those things are difficult, but they are all nevertheless
external. That is, they are in the world about us and attack us
from there rather than being deep within ourselves. Second
Corinthians 12:9 takes us within ourselves to individual deficiencies, personal handicaps, and humiliating limitations, telling us
that God's grace is sufficient for us even in these areas.

A Cruel Theology

A chapter in J. I. Packer's *Knowing God* speaks critically about
what Packer calls the cruelty of a certain kind of gospel ministry.

The chapter is called "These Inward Trials," and the cruelty he discusses is the result of a well-meaning but mistaken theology. It is the teaching that God will save us not only from the punishment due us for sin and the guilt we feel from it, but also from all the burdens, confusions, discouragements, and defeats of this life. As he says, the teaching is usually well-meaning. Its advocates want to commend Christianity. They want to win people to Jesus Christ. But it is also cruel, because the people who teach this way are buying immediate, visible results with false promises. As anyone who has been a Christian for any length of time knows, becoming a Christian does not automatically overcome or eliminate life's difficulties. In fact, it even creates a few that the new Christian did not have before.

And there is this additional cruelty. When people who begin to follow Jesus Christ under a mistaken notion of what being his disciple means face difficulties, even personal failures, they are told by such teachers that the problem is in themselves and to overcome it they need to seek out the secret sins in their lives, confess them, and get right with God again.

It is true, of course, that Christians do sin and that, when we do, we need to confess the sin and turn from it. But that is not the sole or even the major reason for most of life's trials. There are multiple reasons. And if they are wrongly oversimplified in the service of such a cruelly mistaken gospel, the result is either Christians who deny reality, sticking their head in the sand whenever tragedies occur, or else Christians who admit the tragedies of life but blame themselves to the point of undergoing spiritual breakdowns, hysteria, or even (temporary) losses of their faith.

Packer's point is that we have a lot of this type of error today, especially in the "superstar," successful, glamour-oriented approach of much contemporary evangelicalism. It is a dreadful aberration. The proper theological name for it is *triumphalism*.

The Church at Corinth

There were people like this in the church at Corinth, that fellowship of believers located on the narrow isthmus between upper Greece dominated by Athens and the lower portion of Greece dominated by Sparta, which Paul had founded on his second missionary journey. Paul's second letter to the Corinthians has a lot to say about them. Ironically, he calls them "super-apostles" (2 Cor. 11:5). But they were not actually apostles. They were "false apostles, deceitful workmen, masquerading as apostles" (v. 13). They were promoting themselves in order to collect religious followers.

They boasted about their "God-given" visions and revelations. This set them apart, of course. It made them awesome. It gave their words what we would call clout, as it always does when someone says, "God told me so-and-so." To Paul these claims were false, and the type of Christianity they encouraged was both mistaken and harmful. But think what the false apostles would have been saying. They would have pointed to their success and Paul's apparent failure. They would have said things like, "God gives me revelations all the time. Why, just this morning the Lord spoke to me and told me to say what I am about to say to you. What revelations has Paul had in recent years? What visions has he shared with us? As for God's blessing on his work, well, I don't see that God has blessed him very much. In fact, if you look at his career, it seems to be just one great failure or disaster after another."

How does Paul deal with this problem? The way he does it is marvelous and a great example for those who are trying to deal with difficult people as they themselves pursue Christian work.

First, Paul points to what the detractors must have been pointing to as his failures: the beatings he had received, the stoning at Lystra (Acts 14:19), the shipwrecks, the lack of food, clothing, and shelter. "Do you want me to boast like these false apostles?" he seems to be saying. "All right, then, I will boast. But not about my special revelations or God's miraculous interventions in my life. I will boast about my sufferings for his sake. My sufferings are my credentials." The text reads:

> Are they servants of Christ? (I am out of my mind to talk like this.) I am more. I have worked much harder, been in prison more frequently, been flogged more severely, and been exposed to death again and again. Five times I received from the Jews the forty lashes minus one. Three times I was beaten with rods, once I was stoned, three times I was shipwrecked, I spent a night and a day in the open sea, I have been constantly on the move. I have been in danger from rivers, in danger from bandits, in danger from my own countrymen, in danger from Gentiles; in danger in the city, in danger in the country, in danger at sea; and in danger from false brothers. I have labored and toiled and have often gone without sleep; I have known hunger and thirst and have often gone without food; I have been cold and naked. Besides everything else, I face daily the pressure of my concern for all the churches. (2 Cor. 11:23-28)

He concludes, "If I must boast, I will boast of the things that show my weakness" (v. 30). What a contrast to the triumphalism of the false apostles, as well as the many equally mistaken triumphalists today.

Second, Paul mentions a vision the Lord had given him. He does it with great restraint and apparent uneasiness. We know that Paul had received numerous visions because of Luke's reporting of them in the book of Acts (Acts 9:12; 16:9-10; 18:9-10;

22:17-21; 23:11; 27:23-24). The remarkable thing, however, is that in his letters Paul almost never speaks of them. He tells us why here: "There is nothing to be gained" (2 Cor. 12:1). Talking about his visions might add to his prestige, but it would have no benefit at all for the Corinthians. The only thing that would benefit them is careful teaching of the Word of God, which is what Paul actually did instead.

Here he is forced to speak about a vision. He does not want to, but he is driven to it by the foolishness of the Corinthian Christians. Earlier, when the false apostles had boasted of their successes, ironically Paul had boasted of his failures. But he cannot do that here. The opposite of having received a vision is not having received a vision, and Paul could not claim that: first, because it would not have been true (he had received them), and second, because it would have played into the hands of his critics.

So he does speak of a vision. He speaks in the third person, referring to himself as "a man in Christ" whom he knew, a man who was caught up into the third heaven, into Paradise, where he heard inexpressible things that he was not permitted to speak. Obviously, Paul is suggesting that if the false apostles really had been given special revelations by God, they too should have kept silent about them. The very fact that they were speaking about their visions so freely suggests that they were not true visions at all.

The way a ministry should be evaluated is not by claims to special revelations but by faithfulness in preaching and teaching God's Word and by willingness to endure hardships in order to continue doing it.

Paul's Thorn in the Flesh and Ours

At this point Paul must have been embarrassed that he had been forced to mention even this one vision because it is against this background—all I have been describing—that he talks about his thorn in the flesh (v. 7).

What was it? No one knows exactly what it was, though there has been a great deal of speculation, as you might imagine. Since he mentions "flesh" there are people who have supposed this to be a weakness in his moral nature. John Calvin took this view. William Ramsay, the great investigator of Paul's travels, suggested that the thorn was malaria that Paul had picked up in the mosquito-infested swamps of lower, coastal Asia Minor on his first or second missionary journey. Some have suggested epilepsy, which is certainly a physical infirmity. Some have suggested a speech defect because of his admitting to the Corinthians that he did not speak with eloquence when he was among them (1 Cor. 2:1). The explanation that has always appealed to me is that Paul may have had a serious eye infection or condition that restricted his ability to see and brought him personal embarrassment. It is because he seems to have signed his letters personally, after a scribe had taken them down by dictation, but with "large letters" (Gal. 6:11). This might mean that he could not see well and therefore awkwardly copied out the letters of his name. But, of course, it could also mean only that he not been trained to use the fine, cultured letters of a professional writer.

Still others have imagined that Paul was afflicted by guilt over failure to convert his fellow Jews, still others that his thorn was Jewish or Gentile persecution.

As I say, we do not know what this thorn was. But we can probably say that it was physical, the literal meaning of "in my flesh," and that it must have caused Paul great physical torment and embarrassment. In other words, it was a substantial problem and not merely a minor irritation, at least to him. I say this because Paul was a man who willingly put up with all the serious setbacks and sufferings mentioned in chapter 12, not suggesting for a moment that he ever asked for the removal of any of these things. Yet this thorn bothered him so much that in some substantial way he pleaded with the Lord on three separate occasions that it might be removed.

I do not believe it was an oversight on God's part that we have not been told what Paul's affliction was. In my judgment it has been left indefinite so we can identify with him and learn from him, whatever our individual, differing afflictions may be. If Paul's problem was bad eyes, and we were told that this was his thorn, the fact might be comforting for those who have bad eyes. But others would not think about Paul's trouble or be helped by him in this way very much. Since we do not know what he experienced, we can imagine him hurting from what it is that hurts us.

And people do have hurts, even the most triumphant-appearing, victorious Christians or Christian leaders.

Pastors have unusual opportunities to learn of these hurts because the people in their churches often share them and ask for counsel. I have unusual opportunities myself because, in addition to being a pastor of a large inner-city church, I am also a radio pastor to thousands who tune in to the "Bible Study Hour" each week. A radio program is no substitute for regular worship in church. I encourage full church participation. But sometimes people are unable to get to church or attend a church. They are not free to share their burdens with others for one reason or another. Many write to me, and I and the staff of the "Bible Study Hour" pray for them regularly.

Here is a random sampling of things listeners have written to me about.

From a town in Iowa. A family writes that their daughter was diagnosed as having viral encephalitis when she was only twenty days old. She was expected to die quickly because her body was not able to control her body's temperature, but the child lived, though she has been in and out of many hospitals. She is now about eleven years old. This is not all, however. The father suffers from chronic obstructive pulmonary disease, which limits the amount of work he is able to do. He cleans offices part-time. His wife helps, as well as working part time in a school cafeteria. They have other problems, too.

Are they complaining? No. The wife writes, "Please ask God to strengthen us, to fill our hearts with love for him, for one another, and for our fellow humans, and to help us meet these challenges with love, courage, strength, and wisdom."

From a city in Virginia. A wife asks us to pray that God would work in the life of her husband to bring him back home. He has deserted her.

From Kansas. A widow who lives on a pension of less than $1,000 a month and who has lived in her own home for thirty years, writes that she is about to be evicted because of a lawsuit. "Please remember me," she says. "I am so afraid."

From Michigan. A visually handicapped Christian woman is also about to be evicted from her residence. She cannot drive because she cannot see. She has no family, nowhere to go.

From a small town in California. A man writes that he is sixty-one years old and has just lost his job, a frightening thing at that age. He does not even ask for prayer specifically. His letter is a testimony. "I know things are going to be OK. God has supplied and does supply all my needs, and I know he always will."

Many people write about their families, often about unsaved children who are ruining themselves but who will not recognize it, confess their sins, and turn to the Lord. They are a constant grief to their parents, who pray for them earnestly. Sometimes it is an unsaved wife or husband. Sometimes the wife or husband has died. Still other people write of physical suffering. A listener from Montana is dying of cancer and likes the radio because it is the one device she is able to control from her bed even though she cannot raise herself and is always lying down.

This is the kind of thing that I could extend indefinitely, but I have done it enough to make the point. Christians do suffer. God frequently leads even his choice people through deep waters. The Christian life has its thorns.

But that is not all, because it is chiefly to these people (though it is to the rest as well) that our text comes. Paul had a thorn. It was so debilitating that this very godly man, a man who had suffered so much without complaining, asked the Lord on three separate occasions to remove it, and the Lord did not. Instead, he replied in what is surely one of the greatest and most encouraging verses in the Bible, "My grace is sufficient for you, for my power is made perfect in weakness" (2 Cor. 12:9). That is a text for you if you are suffering from some inescapable affliction.

The Lessons of the Thorn

From this lengthy approach, we should now understand well the context for Paul's remarks and understand that many Christians suffer from similar ailments. But from this point we need to explore the text for its lessons about these inescapable burdens. There are at least five of them.

1. Paul's thorn was from Satan.

In a moment we are going to see that Paul's suffering was simultaneously a work of God. The whole point of what Paul is saying depends on the fact that God had his hand on him even in this area. But the fact that God uses evil for his own divine purposes does not mean that evil ceases to be evil or that suffering, which flows from evil and is often caused by it, is not real suffering. Paul makes the nature of the case clear when he speaks of his thorn being "a messenger of Satan, to torment me" (v. 7).

Of all the cruel things that are done to Christians who are

suffering—apart from blaming it on some sin they themselves have committed, which is what Job's comforters tried to do to him—the worst is to minimize or deny the suffering, pretending that it is not really what it is. How easy it is to do that! It is easy to pretend that being confined to a wheelchair is not really very bad, as long as you are not in a wheelchair yourself. It is easy to make light of legal blindness or a loss of hearing, memory, or other faculties, as long as you are not blind, deaf, or otherwise afflicted. It is easy to put on a happy face and paint a rosy picture for the cancer patient, as long as you do not have cancer. But that accomplishes nothing, and it is not genuine Christianity. Christianity faces the evil squarely. Even more than others, Christians believe that this is indeed a genuinely evil and terribly painful world.

2. Paul's thorn was simultaneously from God.

Even though Satan had a hand in Paul's suffering, God was nevertheless ultimately in charge and was responsible. Paul makes this clear in two ways. First, he uses the passive tense to say that the thorn "was given me" (v. 7). It was God who gave it. Second, he says that he prayed to the Lord to take it from him, which would make sense only if God was in control (v. 8).

This is something only Christians can understand. The first point I made, that evil is evil and should not be glibly explained away, is something the world can say, too, though it often doesn't. The world can call evil, evil—particularly if it is in someone else. Only Christians can confess that it is also controlled by God. Why? Because we know it is true, even though we may be at a loss to explain how it is. I say we know this because, even though we may not have been able to see it clearly in our own lives or have experienced it, we have at least seen it in the case of Jesus Christ, our Lord and Savior.

There is no question but that the arrest, trial, and judicial murder of Jesus was a triumph of the most malicious evil. Satan had plotted it, and he accomplished it "with the help of wicked men" (Acts 2:23). Even Jesus called it an "hour . . . when darkness reign[ed]" (Luke 22:53). Yet at the same time, there has never been a moment in history when God was more evidently in charge. All that happened to Jesus happened that the Scripture, which had been given by God beforehand, might be precisely fulfilled. Peter, when he spoke of the Crucifixion at Pentecost, in the same sentence that placed blame squarely on Christ's wicked persecutors, said, "This man was handed over to you by God's set purpose and foreknowledge" (Acts 2:23). Then he quoted texts to show that what happened had been clearly prophesied.

So although we freely confess that we cannot fully understand this or explain why certain things are happening, we say as the framers of the great Westminster Confession of Faith did in classical language: "God from all eternity, did, by his most wise and holy counsel of his own will, freely, and unchangeably ordain whatsoever comes to pass" (chap. 3, par. 1).

3. Because Paul's thorn was simultaneously from God as well as from Satan, it had a divine purpose, and that purpose was ultimately good.

As far as he himself was concerned, the apostle tells us what this good purpose was. It was "to keep me from becoming conceited because of these surpassingly great revelations" (2 Cor. 12:7). And it worked, didn't it? The way he handled the matter of visions and revelations and boastings in this important section of the letter reveals how genuinely humble this great pioneer missionary and apostle had become.

How about you? The purpose of God in your affliction may be quite different. There may be no danger of you becoming proud. Most of us have almost nothing to be proud about. But maybe God is using your suffering as a means of doing good to others, or merely to bring glory to his name.

Take the case of Joseph. Joseph was the envied son of his father, Jacob. He was so hated by his brothers that they actually sold him into slavery. He was taken to Egypt. Although he did well as a slave, even rising to a position of considerable trust and influence, he was falsely accused and eventually cast into the king's prison, where he languished for two long years. This was a "thorn" if there ever was one—many thorns. But God raised Joseph to the highest position in Egypt, short of the Pharaoh's throne itself, and used him to preserve the lives of millions during a great and prolonged famine.

When he met up with his brothers again years later and they were afraid he might take out some cherished revenge upon them, Joseph replied, "Don't be afraid. Am I in the place of God? You intended to harm me [there is that frank facing of evil again], but God intended it for good to accomplish what is now being done, the saving of many lives" (Gen. 50:19-20).

In the cases of Job and the blind man of John 9, who was healed by Jesus, the reason for the afflictions was simply that God might be glorified. So do not despair. The evil in your life is real evil, your suffering real suffering. But God is in control and has a good purpose in all of it, even though you probably cannot see his good purpose now.

4. God's grace was equal to the thorn.

The fourth point is very encouraging, at least to me. For it is the point God himself made in reply to Paul's request to have this painful thorn removed. God did not remove it. He had a purpose for it, as we saw. But he said, "My grace is sufficient for you, for my power is made perfect in weakness" (v. 9).

I find it interesting that Paul, the great apostle, did not even ask for grace. He was asking that the thorn be removed, just as you or I would have asked. Yet God gave him grace anyway. That is, God gave him the necessary strength to live with the difficulty and continue to work and praise God in spite of it. And that is the victory after all, not to escape the suffering, but to triumph in spite of it—particularly since the triumph is not in our own strength but by the grace of God. Sufficient grace? Yes, indeed. If we need sudden grace in some great catastrophe of life, God will supply sudden grace. If it is daily grace we need, God will provide grace day by day. If we need sustaining grace or persevering grace or overcoming grace, that is precisely what we shall have also.

You know how the great hymn "How Firm a Foundation" puts it:

> When through the deep waters I call thee to go,
> The rivers of sorrow shall not overflow,
> For I will be with thee, thy trials to bless,
> And sanctify to thee thy deepest distress.

> When through fiery trials thy pathway shall lie,
> My grace all-sufficient shall be thy supply;
> The flame shall not hurt thee; I only design
> Thy dross to consume, and thy gold to refine.

> E'en down to old age all my people shall prove
> My sovereign, eternal, unchangeable love;
> And when hoary hairs shall their temples adorn,
> Like lambs they shall still in my bosom be borne.

In the midst of his sufferings Job said, "He knows the way that I take; when he has tested me, I will come forth as gold" (Job 23:10).

God's Power in Human Weakness

Paul's last point flows directly from God's special revelation to him. God said, "My power is made perfect in weakness" (v. 9). That is, grace, which provides the power, is seen in us, not when we are strong, but when we are weak. But if that is so, then, as Paul says, "I will boast all the more gladly about my weaknesses, so that Christ's power may rest on me. That is why, for Christ's sake, I delight in weaknesses, in insults, in hardships, in persecutions, in difficulties. For when I am weak, then I am strong" (vv. 9-10).

Do you see how different this is from triumphalism, the point at which we started out? This is not triumphalism, that is, glorying in how successful or victorious or favored a Christian I am. It is the very opposite of triumphalism. It is boasting, yes. But it is boasting in our weaknesses because we know that it is only in our weakness, not our strength, that the power and grace of the Lord Jesus Christ can be seen.

Who is it that you want to glorify? Who do you want to praise? If you want to praise yourself (and have others praise you), then tell us what a wonderful Christian you are. Tell us about your triumphs and victories and visions and revelations. But if that is not your objective, if you want to glorify Jesus rather than yourself, if you want other people to praise him, then do what mature believers in Christ have always done. They do not point to themselves. They point to Jesus. They tell others about his grace, his power, his majesty, his sufficiency, his glory. And when they come into the picture themselves, if they do, they confess only that they are sinners saved by grace. If they are called upon to suffer and do suffer, they do it, not by some great force of character within them, but by the grace and power of him who endured even greater suffering for them, even death on a cross.

"My grace is sufficient for you," God says. Is it sufficient? It is a privilege to be able to show others that it is. So instead of boasting, learn to glory in your weaknesses, since it is only in them that the grace of God is made fully known.

Chapter 13

THE THRONE
OF GRACE

Let us then approach the throne of grace with confidence,
so that we may receive mercy and find grace to help us in
our time of need. HEBREWS 4:16

George Gallup, the founder and director of the Gallup poll organization, has made some interesting studies about the religious life of Americans. His surveys of American religious life are insightful. Recently I came across some remarks he made about prayer. He observed that a great many Americans do pray and even believe in the power of prayer but that there is also evidence that our prayers are extremely superficial. That is, for the most part the prayers of Americans only request things for themselves and contain very little intercession for others, thanksgiving, or requests for forgiveness.

The verse mentioned above is a great verse about prayer, but it is also about grace. In its twenty-seven words, the word *grace* occurs twice. It teaches that God is a God of grace and that we may find grace to help us in every area of need if we will ask God for it.

Prayer Is a Problem

But prayer is a problem, isn't it? When a person becomes a Christian, prayer is one of the things he or she is told about and encouraged to make a part of his or her life, along with regular church attendance and worship, Bible study, fellowship with other Christians, witnessing, and various forms of Christian service. But of all these important things, prayer is actually the hardest to do. We do not have much difficulty coming to church. That involves only a minor reordering of our weekends and a small amount of personal discipline. Bible study is a bit harder; we have to learn how to do it, and we need the will to persevere. Fellowship is natural. Witnessing is natural at first, though often awkward. Service comes naturally. But prayer is in a category by itself. It is neither easy nor natural. Prayer really is a problem.

Why is this? There are a lot of reasons.

1. Many who pray are not Christians.

I began this study by speaking of those who are Christians and of the difficulty they have in praying. But the greatest problem by far is that many try to pray who are not even Christians and that for them prayer is not merely difficult, it is impossible. One writer whose book on prayer I have in my study began it by emphasizing for most of the first chapter that prayer is a natural and universal instinct, particularly when we find ourselves in some difficult spot or danger. I suppose that is true. A drowning man does not need to be told to cry for help. But the cry of the unsaved person is far removed from what true prayer really is and therefore is not really prayer.

Prayer is talking to God. But the unsaved person does not talk to God. He or she does not know God. God is a stranger. Therefore, the person "says a prayer"—haven't you heard that expression?—or only meditates, rather than actually praying.

2. Many of us are too busy.

Another problem we have with prayer is that we are too busy, particularly in our fast-paced society. We use this as an excuse, of course. As an excuse it is invalid. Someone has said, "If you are too busy to pray, you are too busy." That is right. At the height of the Protestant Reformation Martin Luther remarked that he had so much to do in a day that he couldn't get through it unless he spent three or four hours each morning praying. He had the right perspective and had ordered his priorities well. But that is not what I am talking about. I mean only that we live in a fast-paced age and that the pressures of life keep us from thinking about anything very deeply and certainly leave us very little time for any significant spiritual activity.

3. We are too sinful.

This strikes a bit deeper at our problem, though we do not like to admit it. We do not have trouble admitting that we are too busy. On the contrary, we are rather proud of that. We like to be busy. But to admit that we are too sinful and that unconfessed or unrelinquished sin is keeping us from prayer is terrible. Yet that is often the real problem. It was with Israel in the days of Isaiah. God had Isaiah write, "Surely the arm of the LORD is not too short to save, nor his ear too dull to hear. But your iniquities have separated you from your God; your sins have hidden his face from you, so that he will not hear" (Isa. 59:1-2).

That is why real prayer must always include confession. Do you remember the little prayer acrostic using the word *ACTS*? *A* stands for "adoration." We begin by reminding ourselves of who God is and praising him. *C* stands for "confession." One thing God is, is holy. So if we have really stopped to think of who he is and what he is like, we will become conscious of our sin and confess it. After this we have *T*, which stands for "thanksgiving," and *S*, which stands for "supplication" or making requests. In true prayer, supplications come last. Yet this is the point at which most of our prayers begin as well as end.

One specific sin that keeps us from praying, and certainly also keeps us from receiving what we ask for, is an unforgiving spirit. That is why Jesus said, "When you stand praying, if you hold anything against anyone, forgive him, so that your Father in heaven may forgive you your sins" (Mark 11:25).

4. We do not really believe we need it.

When we speak of sin, we are getting close to our problem with prayer, but even so we have not quite hit the target directly, at least in my judgment. Our problem is sin, but above all it is a specific sin, which I would express as a proud self-confidence and self-sufficiency. In other words, it is pride. We do not pray because we do not believe we really need to pray. We think we can do very well by ourselves and in our own ability and strength.

How the devil must laugh at our self-confidence! I think he must look at Americans especially and say something like this: "You Americans are so religious. You have big churches and large budgets. You have so many great religious works. But do you think I care about your big churches and large budgets and many religious works? I have no fear of them at all, as long as you are not praying. In fact, I will even use them to keep you from praying. Ha! Ha! Ha! Build your great church plants. Raise your millions. Start your great evangelistic enterprises. Launch your social programs. They will accomplish no more of lasting spiritual value than the work of secular agencies, and in time I will control them, too, as long as you are not praying. Do you think I fear you? The only one I fear is God, and the only power I fear is his power, which is released through prayer."

Encouragement to Prayer

It is hard to read Hebrews 4:16 against this background without realizing that it is meant to encourage us in prayer. The first way it encourages us is to teach that the throne to which we are invited to come is a throne of grace.

This is not what we first think about when we think about God's throne. The first thing we think about, and rightly, is that it is a throne of terrible judgment. This is what the throne of God stands for in the book of Revelation. As early as the fourth, fifth, and sixth chapters, God is pictured as seated on his throne to execute judgments. These judgments issue from heaven in a series of broken seals, sounding trumpets, and destroying plagues. Then, in chapter 20 before the final vision of the new Jerusalem, the new heaven, and the new earth, comes the judgment pronounced from what is referred to as "a great white throne."

> Then I saw a great white throne and him who was seated on it. Earth and sky fled from his presence, and there was no place for them. And I saw the dead, great and small, standing before the throne, and books were opened. Another book was opened, which is the book of life. The dead were judged according to what they had done as recorded in the books. The sea gave up the dead that were in it, and death and Hades gave up the dead that were in them, and each person was judged according to what he had done. Then death and Hades were thrown into the lake of fire. The lake of fire is the second death. (Rev. 20:11-14)

This is a dreadful scene, one rightly to be feared. But when we come to Hebrews 4:16 we find that it is not a throne of judgment that is presented to us but a throne of grace.

Perhaps, if we know the Bible a bit better, we might think not of the throne of judgment presented in Revelation but the throne of God's holiness described in the sixth chapter of Isaiah. Isaiah had a vision of God "high and exalted." The "train of his robe filled the temple," and there were seraphs who called to one another, "Holy, holy, holy is the LORD Almighty; the whole earth is full of his glory" (v. 3).

The sight of God's throne left Isaiah so overcome by an awareness of his sin that he cried out in anguish, "Woe to me! ... I am ruined! For I am a man of unclean lips, and I live among a people of unclean lips, and my eyes have seen the King, the LORD Almighty" (v. 5). He wanted to flee from God's holy throne. To stand before it was a terrible experience for Isaiah.

But our text is not speaking of a throne of holiness any more than it is speaking of a throne of judgment. It is speaking of a throne of grace.

The God of All Grace

Why is the throne of God described in Hebrews as a throne of grace? The answer is obvious. It is because God is a God of grace. Indeed, he is the God of all grace. It is only in God that true grace may be found.

1. God the Father.

Do you remember how Jesus spoke of God in the Sermon on the Mount? He described him as a Father who is anxious to hear and answer the prayers of his dear children.

> Which of you, if his son asks for bread, will give
> him a stone? Or if he asks for a fish, will give him a
> snake? If you, then, though you are evil, know how
> to give good gifts to your children, how much

more will your Father in heaven give good gifts to
those who ask him! (Matt. 7:9-11)

Some time ago I came across a story told by a missionary who
worked in New York City during the depression. It was Christmas Eve. It was snowing, and he was visiting some of the poorer
families in the neighborhood. He came to one poor apartment,
knocked at the door and, hearing no answer, gently pushed the
door aside and went in. A man was sitting at a broken-down table
in the center of the room, crying. In the corner three little
children lay sleeping on a straw mat. The man explained that he
had lost his job several months earlier, that his wife had died the
year before, and that the children had gone to sleep knowing that
the next day was Christmas, expecting that Santa Claus would
come to fill the stockings they had hung up earlier that evening
with innocent expectations. The man was crying because he had
absolutely no money and not a thing to give them.

Jesus was saying that if a good earthly father is like that,
certainly God, who is a most gracious heavenly Father, will hear
and answer the prayers of his dear children.

When I came across that story, my mind went back to an
analogous story from my own childhood. It is one of my very best
childhood memories. My father was released from military service in World War II in the third week of December 1945, and
our family immediately started north from Barksdale Field, Lou-
isiana, where we had been stationed, to McKeesport, Pennsylvania, where we had relatives and hoped to stay while my father
found a job at the local hospital. We were trying to make Mc-
Keesport by Christmas Eve, and my aunt and grandmother, who
were expecting us, had everything ready for a very joyful Christmas.

We weren't able to make it. On the way north through the
mountains of West Virginia we ran into a terrible snowstorm. I
remember how the car got stuck on a steep mountain upgrade

and how we almost slid over an embankment at one point. At last, late on Christmas Eve night, my parents realized that we would never get home and so checked us into one small room of a small hotel in a mountain village. I had two sisters then. So there were three children, and we were all very disappointed that we had not gotten through to McKeesport for Christmas. We were worried that Santa Claus would miss us, too, because he would not be able to find us. Nevertheless, we hopefully hung our stockings from the top drawer of an old wood dresser.

The next morning we were thrilled to find our stockings filled with Life Savers, chewing gum, and candy. My parents had very little money at that time, and they were surely exhausted from the rapid packing, hurried trip, and difficult snowstorm. But they didn't want to disappoint us. I realized later that they must have gone out late that night, after we had gone to sleep, to get what they could to meet our childish expectations. That is a happy memory for me, as I said. But Jesus is saying that if earthly parents can be like that, sinful and imperfect as we all are, how much more gracious and able to meet our needs is God, our heavenly Father.

2. God the Son.

It is not only God the Father who is gracious, however. It is God the Son, too. Jesus is as much the God of grace as is his Father. This is the point the author of Hebrews is making in chapter 4. He has introduced Jesus as our great High Priest, a theme he is going to develop in a variety of ways throughout the book. But as he begins he emphasizes that he is a High Priest who has become a man like us and who is able to understand and sympathize with us in our problems. The verse immediately before our text on prayer says, "For we do not have a high priest who is unable to sympathize with our weaknesses, but we have one who has been tempted in every way, just as we are—yet was without sin" (v. 15).

The New International Version is very good at this point, an improvement on the earlier versions. For the point is not that Jesus was tempted in every way we are, that is, that he endured all the varieties of all the temptations we experience. It is rather that he was tempted in all sorts of ways, just as we are tempted in all sorts of ways. In other words, he knows what temptation is like. Therefore, he understands us and sympathizes with us when we are tempted.

We are here reminded of Jesus' temptation by Satan during the forty days he spent in the wilderness following his baptism by John. There were three temptations, and they were representative. The first was to use his divine power to turn stones into bread. It appealed to his senses. He was hungry. The second was to use worldly means to achieve success and gain power. It appealed to his intellect. The third was a spiritual trial, the devil promising to give him the kingdoms of the world and their glory if only he would fall down and worship Satan. We have equivalent temptations in the areas of our physical bodies, our minds, and our spiritual consciousness or desires.

Jesus also experienced earthly trials. For example, he was poor. He had no home. He was often hungry and thirsty. He was misunderstood, abused, and slandered. He was rejected by those close to him, even his immediate family. He was betrayed by one of his disciples and denied by Peter, one of his closest friends.

If that were not enough to prove the author of Hebrews' claim that Jesus is able to sympathize with us, we need only remember that he was forsaken by his Father during the moments when he hung upon the cross and was made sin for us. This was such an acute agony for him that he cried out despairingly, "My God, my God, why have you forsaken me?" (Matt. 27:46). Remember that the next time you feel that God has turned his back on you, that he is not listening to your prayers, that he has abandoned you. You are not really abandoned. God hears you even when you are certain he does not. But Jesus *was* forsaken, and because of it, he understands exactly what you are feeling. He is able to help you in your despair.

3. God the Holy Spirit.

The Holy Spirit is also gracious. That is one reason he is called the Counselor (John 14:16, 25; 15:26; 16:7). The Greek word is *parakletos*. It is a rich word rightly translated "helper," "advocate," "comforter," and "counselor," meaning that the Holy Spirit also strengthens us and pleads for us. But the Holy Spirit is certainly a comfort, too, as any believer who has gone through difficult times surely knows. We sing,

> Come, dearest Lord, descend and dwell
> By faith and love in every breast;
> Then we shall know and taste and feel
> The joys that cannot be expressed.

Our triune God is the God of all grace, and each member of the Godhead has a part in hearing and answering prayer. We customarily say that prayer is made *to* God the Father, *through* the Lord Jesus Christ, and *in* the Holy Spirit.

A Way Opened to God

When we are talking about prayer and speak of God's throne being a throne of grace and of the triune God being a God of grace, we have to go a bit further and add that it is also the grace of God in Jesus Christ that has made prayer possible. Or to put it another way, it is because of his great grace that God has opened the way to his throne by Jesus Christ.

A little later on in Hebrews, in chapter 9, the author spells out the meaning of Christ's work by reference to the ark of the covenant. The ark of the covenant was the sole piece of furniture kept in the Most Holy Place of the Jewish temple. It was a box about a yard long and a foot and a half high and deep, and it was covered with gold. Its lid was pure gold, and it was used to hold the stone tablets of the law of Moses. On top of the lid were two golden figures of cherubim or angels. They faced each other, and God was understood to dwell symbolically in the space between their outstretched wings. In this picture, judgment is represented. For as God looks down on mankind from between the outstretched wings of the cherubim, what he sees is the law of Moses, which each of us has broken. In this form, the lid of the ark functioned as the judgment seat of God.

But the lid was not called the judgment seat. It was called the mercy seat. This is because once a year, on the Day of Atonement, after the high priest had sacrificed an animal for the sin of the people of Israel, the priest brought the blood of that slain animal into the Most Holy Place and sprinkled it on the mercy seat. Now the Ark was no longer a picture of judgment, the holiness of God pouring forth to consume the sinner. Instead it was a picture of grace. The throne of judgment became a throne of grace—because now the blood of the innocent sacrifice, slain for the sins of the people, has intervened.

This is a wonderful picture of what Jesus Christ has done. Only in this case, he is both the sacrifice and the High Priest. And his sacrifice of himself is not merely a symbol, meaningful but unable to take away sin. It is the true atoning sacrifice to which the symbolism pointed. It is he who has made the throne of judgment a throne of grace and by his death opened the way to God for all who will come through faith in that sacrifice.

The author of Hebrews says in reference to the Old Testament priests, "Unlike the other high priests, he does not need to offer sacrifices day after day, first for his own sins, and then for the sins of the people. He sacrificed for their sins once for all when he offered himself" (Heb. 7:27).

Again, "He [Christ] entered the Most Holy Place once for all by his own blood, having obtained eternal redemption" (Heb. 9:12).

And again, "Just as man is destined to die once, and after that to face judgment, so Christ was sacrificed once to take away the sins of many people; and he will appear a second time, not to bear sin, but to bring salvation to those who are waiting for him" (vv. 27-28).

Drawing Near in Confidence

The bottom line of this discussion is that, because of who God is and what Jesus Christ has done in dying for us, changing the throne of judgment into a throne of grace, we who trust Christ are to draw near the throne of grace in confidence. If we came in our own merit, we could have no confidence at all. The throne of God would be a place of terror. But since God has done what was needed to take away all judgment for our sin, it is now sin for us to come in any other way but with confidence. If we come in confidence, we can come knowing that God will do exactly what the author of Hebrews says he will do and we will indeed "find grace to help us in our time of need."

Whatever our need may be! Do you seek forgiveness for sin? You will find God's grace forgiving you for every sin. Do you need strength for daily living? You will find the grace of God providing strength. Do you need comfort because of some great loss? God will provide comfort. Direction for some important decision? You will receive direction. Encouragement? You will receive encouragement. Wisdom? That too.

Remember what Paul wrote in Romans 8. "If God is for us, who can be against us? He who did not spare his own Son, but gave him up for us all—how will he not also, along with him, graciously give us all things?" (vv. 31-32). Charles Wesley must have been thinking of this when he wrote,

> Arise, my soul, arise, shake off thy guilty fears;
> The bleeding Sacrifice in my behalf appears;
> Before the throne my Surety stands;
> My name is written on his hands.
>
> Five bleeding wounds he bears, received on Calvary;
> They pour effectual prayers, they strongly plead for me;
> "Forgive him, O forgive," they cry,
> "Nor let that ransomed sinner die!"
>
> My God is reconciled; his pardoning voice I hear;
> He owns me for his child, I can no longer fear;
> With confidence I now draw nigh,
> And "Father, Abba, Father!" cry.

So pray! That is what we need to do. We do not need more lessons on prayer or elaborate instructions on how to pray. What we need to do is pray. So pray! The Bible says, "You do not have, because you do not ask God" (James 4:2). Jesus said, "Ask and it will be given to you; seek and you will find; knock and the door will be opened to you" (Matt. 7:7).

On one occasion Jesus told a story about prayer.

> In a certain town there was a judge who neither feared God nor cared about men. And there was a widow in that town who kept coming to him with the plea, "Grant me justice against my adversary."
>
> For some time he refused. But finally he said to himself, "Even though I don't fear God or care about men, yet because this widow keeps bothering me, I will see that she gets justice, so that she won't eventually wear me out with her coming!" . . .

> Listen to what the unjust judge says. And will
> not God bring about justice for his chosen ones,
> who cry out to him day and night? Will he keep
> putting them off? I tell you, he will see that they
> get justice, and quickly. (Luke 18:2-8)

The point of the story is not that God is indifferent or hard of hearing or difficult to be entreated. It is just the opposite. God is not indifferent. He hears each and every one of our cries. He has opened the way and is easy to approach through Jesus Christ. He does not always answer as we expect or according to our timetables, of course. His ways are not our ways; nor are his thoughts our thoughts (cf. Isa. 55:8). But he welcomes our prayers and delights to answer them.

So why do we not pray? Can it be that we do not really believe that God is like this? Or do we just not believe we need his help?

Our text says,

> Therefore, since we have a great high priest who
> has gone through the heavens, Jesus the Son of
> God, let us hold firmly to the faith we profess. For
> we do not have a high priest who is unable to sym-
> pathize with our weaknesses, but we have one who
> has been tempted in every way, just as we are—yet
> was without sin. Let us then approach the throne
> of grace with confidence, so that we may receive
> mercy and find grace to help us in our time of
> need. (Heb. 4:14-16)

Abundant grace from the throne of grace.
It is exactly what we need.

Chapter 14

THE GRACE OF GIVING

And now, brothers, we want you to know about the grace that God has given the Macedonian churches. 2 CORINTHIANS 8:1

We have been discussing some very practical matters in these studies, but it is hard to imagine a more practical matter than our giving to God, specifically giving money to support spiritual causes. Most Christians understand they are to do this. But what might be surprising to most is associating giving with grace, which is what this chapter is about. The duty of giving is understood, perhaps even the satisfaction or joy of giving. But "the grace of giving"? That combination of words probably seems strange to most persons.

Three things are implied by this title. *First*, giving is a privilege given to Christians by God—a privilege, because it is a way in which we become partners with God in assuring that the gospel and its benefits are made known to other people.

Second, the disposition to give to spiritual causes is itself a grace-gift from God. Left to ourselves, we would never have this desire. But when God begins to work in our lives to make us like Jesus Christ, one thing he does is begin to make us generous with our money, knowing that where our treasure is, there will our hearts be also (cf. Matt. 6:21).

Third, giving is a natural response of gratitude to God's prior grace toward us in Christ and the gospel.

Each of these ideas lies behind or is explicitly stated in the eighth and ninth chapters of 2 Corinthians, two chapters that contain the most extensive treatment in the Bible of the principles that should govern Christian giving. Paul repeatedly mentions grace in these chapters. He does so at the start of chapter 8: "And now, brothers, we want you to know about the *grace* that God has given the Macedonian churches" (2 Cor. 8:1). That is his introduction to the subject. He continues, "So we urged Titus, since he had earlier made a beginning, to bring also to completion this act of *grace* on your part" (v. 6). He concludes with the challenge: "See that you also excel in this *grace* of giving" (v. 7). Each of these verses presents giving as a grace of God.

But then the word is also used of Jesus Christ and his gift of himself for us: "For you know the grace of our Lord Jesus Christ, that though he was rich, yet for your sakes he became poor, so that you through his poverty might become rich" (v. 9). At the end of chapter 9 Paul speaks in the same way of "the surpassing grace God has given you," by which he means God's gift of Jesus to be our Savior (2 Cor. 9:14).

Finally, Paul is also speaking of giving in the middle of chapter 9 when he says, "God is able to make all grace abound to you, so that in all things at all times, having all that you need, you will abound in every good work. As it is written: 'He has scattered abroad his gifts to the poor; his righteousness endures forever'" (vv. 8-9).

In these two important chapters on giving the word *grace* occurs six times.

The Churches of Macedonia and Corinth

The background to these chapters is important for understanding them. Famine had come to lands lying at the far eastern end of the Mediterranean Sea, and the Christians in Jerusalem were suffering because of it. Paul was not there. He was traveling among the Gentiles in order to plant churches in Asia Minor, Macedonia, and Greece. But he saw the need of the Jerusalem church as an opportunity to demonstrate the unity of all believers in Christ. He decided to do this by receiving an offering for the Jerusalem church from the Gentiles. We learn from 1 Corinthians 16 that he began this project in Galatia, and from 2 Corinthians 8 we learn that he had pursued it in among the poverty-stricken churches of Macedonia.

In 1 Corinthians 16 and 2 Corinthians 8–9, he is urging participation in this offering by the Christians at Corinth.

The problem was that the Corinthians had not followed through on their original early commitment to share in this offering. They seemed to have been willing at first. But like many of us, they had let the matter of their giving to God's work slide. Now Paul was sending Titus, one of his faithful fellow-workers and companions, along with two other unnamed brothers to receive this offering, and he was writing to assure that the Corinthians would actually take the offering and have it waiting when Titus and his companions arrived.

Anyone who has ever tried to get someone else to give to religious or charitable causes knows how difficult motivating another person can be. So we are wise to ask: How does Paul move the Corinthians to be faithful in this area? It is noteworthy that he does not nag, scold, beg, or plead. But neither is he against using some very direct motivation. If we read the chapters carefully, we will find him appealing to the need for personal consecration on the Corinthians' part, the example of Christ, the love and grace of God for us, and even to a bit of proper pride and self-interest.

The chief element in Paul's attempt to motivate the Corinthians to great giving was the example of the poorer churches of Macedonia. Paul had visited this area on his second missionary journey, when he had founded churches in Philippi, Thessalonica, and other cities. The members of these churches had been generous. Years later, when he wrote to the Philippian Christians, Paul acknowledged that "when I set out from Macedonia, not one church shared with me in the matter of giving and receiving, except you only; for even when I was in Thessalonica, you sent me aid again and again when I was in need" (Phil. 4:15-16). This means that the Christians in Philippi had given to his support at least four times: once when he started out; twice when he was in Thessalonica; and a fourth time when he was in Rome, since the letter to the Philippians was written in part to thank them for it. We know from 2 Corinthians 11:9 that the Macedonians also gave at least once more when Paul first came to Corinth.

So Paul is seeking to motivate by another's good example, and his first example of generous giving is the churches of Macedonia.

God's Formula for Great Giving

But these were poor churches, as I said a moment ago. Corinth was a thriving, prosperous place by comparison. How is it that the poorer Macedonian churches had been able to set such a good example for the church at Corinth? The first answer to this question is in 2 Corinthians 8:2. I call it "God's Formula for Great Giving." It says, "Out of the most severe trial, their overflowing joy and their extreme poverty welled up in rich generosity." Here are three elements: (1) a severe trial, (2) overflowing joy, and (3) extreme poverty. Combined, says Paul, they produced generosity of a rich and exemplary kind.

1. A severe trial.

We do not know what this severe trial was. It may have been persecution. It may have been the poverty Paul openly acknowledges to have been theirs. Whatever it was, it represented less than ideal circumstances, indeed, circumstances we might call very grim in nature.

Isn't it strange that this should be a factor in the extraordinary giving of these churches? It is not the way we would expect things to be. We usually think the opposite. We think that if a person is going through some trial, his or her attention should rightly be directed to that problem and not to the needs of other people. That is how we would expect to react ourselves. But here, as in so many areas of life, Christian experience is entirely different from what we would expect. Unlike other people, when Christians go through trials they think about others who are also suffering, and they reach out to them.

Do we need an example? The best example is Jesus, who, when he was hanging on the cross, was not thinking about himself first. He thought of the soldiers ("Father, forgive them, for they do not know what they are doing," Luke 23:34), his mother ("Dear woman, here is your son," John 19:26) and the dying thief ("I tell you the truth, today you will be with me in paradise," Luke 23:43).

2. Overflowing joy.

In what were the Macedonian Christians joyful? Paul does not say, but we may suppose their joy came from several things. They would have had joy in salvation itself, for Paul writes in 1 Thessalonians how the believers there welcomed the message with the *joy* given by the Holy Spirit (1 Thess. 1:6). Before the coming of the gospel they were lost in heathen darkness and were, like Paul describes the Ephesians to have been before their conversion, "without hope and without God in the world" (Eph. 2:12). After they had believed, they were conscious of having found God and of having passed out of darkness into light. In the second chapter of 1 Thessalonians Paul speaks of the Thessalonians being his "hope," *"joy,"* and "crown" (v. 19) and in the next verse as his "glory and *joy"* (v. 20). We may assume that the Thessalonians thought of him that way too.

Similarly, in Philippians Paul speaks explicitly of the believers' *"joy* in Christ Jesus" (Phil. 1:26), and he urges them to "rejoice in the Lord always" (Phil. 4:4), that is, to continue as they were doing. Commentators have often observed that joy is a dominant note in this letter.

Every Christian should be joyful. But we are concerned with the link between joy and giving, and one thing joy must indicate in this context is that the giving of the Macedonians was unconstrained. That is, it was of their own free will, and that is why it was joyful. As long as our giving is constrained, as it is when we give our taxes to the government, it is a burden and is frequently coupled with resentment. But when we give freely, as we ought to do for Christian causes, we give joyfully and our joy is enhanced by the giving.

I think here of Frances Ridley Havergal, who wrote lines we often sing with little understanding or commitment:

> Take my silver and my gold,
> Not a mite would I withhold.

Those lines were autobiographical. That is, Frances Havergal did what she described. We know from her writings that at the time she wrote those words she sent to the Church Missionary Society all her gold and silver jewelry, including a jewel chest that she described as being fit for a countess. She wrote to a close friend, "I don't need to tell you that I never packed a box with such pleasure." That is a joy generous Christians recognize. They know that joy leads to generous giving, as our text in 2 Corinthians teaches, and that it is enhanced by it.

3. Extreme poverty.

The third element in this formula for generous giving is poverty, indeed, extreme poverty. Again, what an utterly contrary principle from what the world teaches! If you are trying to raise large sums of money for a secular charity and if you hire a fund-raising organization to assist in the campaign, you will be told that the first third of the goal must be raised by advance gifts from large donors, the second third by nearly as large gifts from wealthy people, and only the last third from your organization's regular constituency. Or, depending on the cause, the expectations may be even more disproportionate. Sometimes the gifts from large donors are supposed to be at least 80 percent of the whole.

That is not how it is in Christian circles. Large gifts have their place, perhaps to launch a new project or pay for a special need. But by and large, the work of the church is sustained, and sustained very well, by the regular small gifts of those who are not wealthy. In fact, in many places the spreading of the gospel is underwritten mostly by the very poor.

Some time ago I came across some statistics that showed that giving among the very poor is remarkable. In the United States those below the poverty line give about 5 percent of their income to charitable causes. Those who are in the middle income brackets give slightly more, about 7 percent, because they have more from which to give. But when people move into the higher brackets, that is, above $100,000 per year, the rate falls back to only 2 percent. So, statistically, it is usually not the rich who give generously but those who are not nearly so well off.

The Macedonians were poor. Paul says that they were in "extreme poverty." Therefore, their giving must have been sacrificial, as all truly great giving is.

Don't you think that the giving of the poor widow whom Jesus saw casting two very small copper coins into the temple treasury was sacrificial? Of course, it was! Jesus said of her, "This poor widow has put in more than all the others. All these people gave their gifts out of their wealth; but she out of her poverty put in all she had to live on" (Luke 21:3-4). Do not think that she was unhappy doing it. Jesus did not mention her joy. He was speaking of how God evaluated the gift. But even though he did not mention it, we can be sure that the widow was a joyful giver.

Here is another example. Gordon, the English general, was a godly man who attributed his military success to God. When the British government wanted to honor him he declined all money and titles. The only thing he accepted was a gold medal that had been inscribed with a record of his thirty-three military campaigns. It was his most prized possession. After his death this famous medal could not be found. Where was it? Eventually it was learned that Gordon had sent it to the city of Manchester during a severe famine so it could be melted down and the gold used to buy food for those who were starving. In his diary under the date on which he mailed the medal were the words: "The last earthly thing I had in this world that I valued I have given to the Lord Jesus Christ."

The result of this unusual combination of circumstances was great giving. It was according to the formula: A severe trial plus overflowing joy plus extreme poverty equals rich generosity. How does that add up? Isn't that like saying, "Minus one, plus minus fifteen, plus minus three equals a million"? Yes, it is. But that is God's arithmetic, strange as it may seem to us. It is the grace of giving, and it works.

The Secret of Great Giving (2 Cor. 8:5)

Verse 5 adds a further explanation of the remarkable giving of the Macedonian Christians: "And they did not do as we expected, but they gave themselves first to the Lord and then to us in keeping with God's will." I call this a further explanation of the grace of giving because, as we well know, trials and poverty do not in themselves produce great giving, not even among Christians necessarily. In fact, they sometimes do the opposite. They sometimes produce bitterness in people who thereby become self-centered, mean, tight-fisted, and greedy.

In this verse Paul explains that the Macedonian Christians had: (1) first given themselves to the Lord, and (2) then given themselves to himself and the missionary team that came with him.

1. Given to the Lord.

It is hard to emphasize this too much because in the fullest sense everything in the Christian life begins, continues, and ends with this necessity. It begins here because this is what it means to be a Christian. To be a Christian is to surrender oneself to Jesus Christ, repenting of sin, believing on him, and beginning to follow him as one's Master. It continues here because Jesus calls us to a life of discipleship, which means serving him as Lord of our entire life. It ends here because Christians must persevere in their original calling to the very end.

Some years ago I heard a prominent member of a board of directors of an organization say, "To be a good board member you should be able to give one of three things: time, talent, or wealth." That is good worldly wisdom. But a Christian will do better. A Christian will give everything he or she is or has to Jesus Christ.

Right here is why so many believers know so little about the grace of giving. They know the gospel. They believe it. But they have not really given themselves to God, at least not wholeheartedly. They are like Jacob when he stood on the banks of the Jabbok on the edge of Esau's territory. Twenty years earlier he had cheated his brother out of his father Isaac's blessing. Esau had threatened to kill him, and he had been forced to flee across the desert to live with his uncle Laban. As the twenty years passed, he gradually forgot about Esau's threats. But when he finally left Laban to return home and was getting close to where Esau lived, he began to remember Esau and became very afraid. What if Esau had not forgotten? What if he was still determined to kill him?

When Jacob got to the edge of Esau's territory, he decided to send a servant ahead of him to tell Esau he was coming and get a feeling for how he would most likely be received. The servant came back with the report, "Esau . . . is coming to meet you, and four hundred men are with him" (Gen. 32:6). To Jacob this was a vast army, and he could only assume the worst. He had to believe that Esau was going to attack him and his small band of servants. So he divided his company into two parts, saying, "If Esau comes and attacks one group, the group that is left may escape" (v. 8).

Ah, but what if he was in the group Esau attacked?

As Jacob thought it over he decided that something more drastic was necessary. He decided to appease Esau with gifts. He took two hundred female goats and sent them ahead of him across the barren terrain toward Esau and his approaching army. He put a servant in charge of the goats and gave him these instructions: "When my brother Esau meets you and asks, 'To whom do you belong, and where are you going, and who owns all these animals in front of you?' then you are to say, 'They belong to your servant Jacob. They are a gift sent to my lord Esau, and he is coming behind us'" (vv. 17-18).

After he had sent the servant with the female goats, Jacob sent another servant with twenty male goats, giving him the same instructions. He said to himself, "I will pacify him with these gifts I am sending on ahead" (v. 20).

After that he sent:

> thirty female camels with their young,
> followed By Forty Cows,
> ten Bulls,
> twenty Female Donkeys, and
> ten male donkeys.

Each of these groups of animals was tended by a servant who was to tell Esau that the animals were a present from Jacob to him. It was a hilarious picture, all the possessions of Jacob strung out across the desert in groups moving toward Esau.

He went even further. After he had dispatched the animals, he sent his family ahead, choosing Leah, the least favored wife, to go first together with her children, then Rachel, the favored wife, with her children. And there at last, with his family and possessions sent ahead of him across the desert toward Esau, was Jacob. He was standing on the edge of the Jabbok, all alone and trembling.

I suppose that if he had known the hymn Christians used to sing some years ago, he might have sung, "I surrender all . . . all the goats, all the sheep, all the camels, all the cows, all the bulls, all the donkeys, even my wives and children." But he had not surrendered himself. The text says, "So Jacob's gifts went on ahead of him, but he himself spent the night in the camp" (v. 21).

That night the angel of God came and wrestled with him and brought him to the point of personal surrender.

Maybe the angel needs to wrestle with you. You have been stingy in your support of the Lord's work, giving only as much as you felt compelled to give. When the Lord pressed the claims of his work upon you, you responded by giving up a few goats. When he pressed you further you gave him a few sheep, then camels, then cows. You sang, "I surrender all the donkeys." You were even willing to give your wife or husband or children. But you have never surrendered yourself. If you have not done that, you need to do it. You need to do it now. There is no substitute for giving yourself to the Lord. You will never know the joy of the grace of giving (or any other grace) until you do.

2. Given to Paul and his team.

The second thing Paul says in order to explain the extraordinary giving of the Macedonians is that, having first given themselves to the Lord, they then also gave themselves to him and his missionary team. But that is not really a great additional achievement. It is something that follows naturally from having first given ourselves to the Lord. It is an inevitable sequence. If we give ourselves to God, we will give ourselves to others. This is because we will want to serve God with our whole selves, and the only way to serve God is by serving other people.

The Greatest Example of Great Giving

When I began to write about the giving of the churches of Macedonia I said that this was Paul's first motivating example of great giving. It was a good one, as you can see. But there is also a second great example of great giving, and that is the giving by Jesus of himself to be our Savior. Paul writes of it in 2 Corinthians 8:9 when he says, "For you know the grace of our Lord Jesus Christ, that though he was rich, yet for your sakes he became poor, so that you through his poverty might become rich."

The giving of the Macedonians was great, but the giving of the Lord Jesus Christ was greater still, and we can be sure that it was the example of his giving that motivated them, as it has so many Christians.

There are four stages in this verse, two that concern the Lord Jesus and two that concern ourselves. Stage number one: Christ's riches. Before the Incarnation, when he was in the presence of the Father in heaven, Jesus was rich with all the riches of the Godhead. Everything in heaven and earth was his. Stage number two: Christ's poverty. Jesus laid all this aside in order to become a man and die on the cross for our salvation. Paul describes his sacrifice in classic language in Philippians.

> Who, being in very nature God, did not consider equality with God something to be grasped, but made himself nothing, taking the very nature of a servant, being made in human likeness. And being found in appearance as a man, he humbled himself and became obedient to death—even death on a cross! (Phil. 2:6-8)

Never in the entire history of the universe did anyone abandon so much in order to become so poor for so many.

But it was not for nothing, for the third and fourth stages of verse 9 explain how we have benefited from Christ's giving. Stage number three: Our poverty. We possess nothing of any spiritual value. We have nothing in ourselves that can commend us to God. In fact, we are guilty of the precise opposite. There is much to condemn us. But then, stage number four: Our riches. Because of Jesus' gift of himself, we who have nothing and are nothing are lifted from the depths of our sin and misery and are made objects of God's great grace and coheirs with Jesus Christ of God's riches.

Shouldn't the example of Jesus, who freely gave himself for us, move us to great giving for others? It should, or we do not understand the gospel.

I heard of a man who was on a pulpit committee who did not understand it. He was sent to hear a man who was a candidate for the empty pulpit of his church, and afterward he reported back to the committee: "The candidate had a three-point sermon on stewardship. The points were: (1) Earn all you can, (2) Save all you can, (3) Give all you can."

"How was the message?" the other members of the committee asked him.

"The first two points were excellent, but the third point spoiled it all," he replied.

Great giving is motivated above all by the Cross of Christ. Early in the nineteenth century King Frederick William III of Prussia was carrying on expensive wars intended to make a great nation of the Prussian people. He did not have enough money for his campaigns. So he hit upon this idea. He asked the women of Prussia to bring their gold and silver jewelry to be melted down and made into money so their country could buy instruments of war. At the same time Frederick determined that for each gift of gold or silver he would give in return an iron decoration bearing the inscription, "I gave gold for iron, 1813."

The response was overwhelming, and the people who received their gifts from the king prized them even more than their former possessions. In fact, for a time it became fashionable for women to wear no jewelry. They wore their iron decorations instead. So it was that the Order of the Iron Cross, the most exalted decoration of the German people, was established. Those who are members of this order wear no other decorations, only this cross.

We need a generation of people who have become members of the Order of the Cross of Jesus Christ, people who have given everything to him because he first loved us and gave himself for us. It will be these people who will have received the grace of giving.

Chapter 15

GRACE, SEASONED WITH SALT

---

*Let your conversation be always full of grace, seasoned
with salt, so that you may know how to answer everyone.*

COLOSSIANS 4:6

A number of years ago I became fascinated with the writings
of Neil Postman, a professor of communication arts at New
York University and author of a best-selling critique of our
television-saturated society, *Amusing Ourselves to Death: Public Discourse in the Age of Show Business.* One of my friends on
the West Coast knew of this interest and sent me an article
about Postman from *Harper's* magazine (March 1991). Actually it was about two people: Postman, who criticizes television, and a woman named Camille Paglia, who is a defender
of it. Mrs. Paglia is also a professor, a teacher of humanities
at Philadelphia College of the Arts. The article was a polished
transcript of a conversation between these two very fascinating people.

But here is the delightful thing. The magazine's editors
had arranged this conversation around a four-star dinner

213

served in the private Tasting Room of New York City's Le Bernardin restaurant, whose chef is Gilbert Le Coze. The editors had invited them to come to the restaurant to eat and talk. So as we were being told what they said, we were also told what they were eating. There would be an argument by Paglia. Then, for example,

. . . baked sea urchin . . .

After this there would be a further exchange between the two popular authors, followed by

. . . shrimp and basil beignets . . .

In the course of this lively conversation the two dining companions enjoyed seared scallops in truffle vinaigrette, black bass in coriander nage, roast monkfish on savoy cabbage, and at the end a carousel of caramel desserts. I was as fascinated with the dinner as with the conversation.

Which was exactly the point, of course. For the setting was a device the editors had for indicating that the conversation between Postman and Paglia was well prepared, satisfying, and extremely tasty.

Which also makes it a good introduction to our text, a verse in which the apostle Paul applies the need for grace to the speech or conversation of Christians, using a gastronomic image: "Let your conversation be always full of grace, seasoned with salt, so that you may know how to answer everyone" (Col. 4:6). In this verse the word translated "conversation" is the common Greek word *logos*, usually translated "word" in other passages. So the verse is talking about the importance of our words or speech, and it is telling us that our speech should be gracious and not insipid to the taste. It should be well seasoned.

Evil Heart, Evil Tongue

Gracious speech flows from a heart that has been established in the grace of God. Gracious speech does not flow naturally from a sinful heart. But that is what we are all born with, according to the Bible. Jeremiah described the unregenerate heart by saying, "The heart is deceitful above all things and beyond cure. Who can understand it?" (Jer. 17:9).

This is the state of every heart apart from the grace of God in Jesus Christ, and a heart like this speaks harmful, deceitful words because it is exactly that, harmful and deceitful.

As I began to research this subject I found two things: (1) not many contemporary writers have dealt with the importance of how we speak, whether graciously or not, and (2) the Bible has a lot to say about human words and conversation. Do you know that the very first mention of "words" in the Bible is in Genesis 4:23, where the evil despot Lamech is said to have used "words" to boast about having killed another man? His words are in verse, which makes this the first recorded poem in human history.

> Adah and Zillah, listen to me; wives of Lamech,
> hear my words. I have killed a man for wounding
> me, a young man for injuring me. If Cain is
> avenged seven times, then Lamech seventy-seven
> times. (vv. 23-24)

And it doesn't get better after that. In Psalm 55:20-21, David speaks of the man who attacks his friends, saying of him, "His speech is smooth as butter, yet war is in his heart." Psalm 64 speaks of people "who sharpen their tongues like swords and aim their words like deadly arrows" (v. 3). Psalm 94:4 speaks of evil men's "arrogant words," and Psalm 109:3 of hateful words ("words of hatred"). The author of Proverbs says, "The words of the wicked lie in wait for blood, but the speech of the upright rescues them" (Prov. 12:6) and "Reckless words pierce like a sword" (Prov. 12:18).

It is the same in the New Testament. Peter is concerned about false teachers who harm their listeners by words:

> They mouth empty, boastful words and, by appealing to the lustful desires of sinful human nature, they entice people who are just escaping from those who live in error. They promise them freedom, while they themselves are slaves of depravity. (2 Pet. 2:18-19)

Jude reminds us of "all the harsh words ungodly sinners have spoken against [God]" (v. 15).

This is a problem for Christians, too, though it should not be. James writes about it in the third chapter of his very practical letter, warning Christians that their tongues are unruly by nature and can be quite dangerous.

> When we put bits into the mouths of horses to make them obey us, we can turn the whole animal. Or take ships as an example. Although they are so large and are driven by strong winds, they are steered by a very small rudder wherever the pilot wants to go. Likewise the tongue is a small part of the body, but it makes great boasts. Consider what a great forest is set on fire by a small spark. The tongue also is a fire, a world of evil among the parts of the body. It corrupts the whole person, sets the whole course of his life on fire, and is itself set on fire by hell.

All kinds of animals, birds, reptiles, and creatures of the sea are being tamed and have been tamed by man, but no man can tame the tongue. It is a restless evil, full of deadly poison (James 3:3-8).

The picture James gives is not overdrawn. We can think easily of people who have stirred the world to great harm by their words. Hitler is a prime example, and there have been other similar demagogues throughout human history. Whole nations, whole decades have literally been set on fire by the tongue. And James is right in something else, too: "No man can tame the tongue." The tongue is incorrigible. But "what is impossible with men is possible with God" (Luke 18:27). God can tame it. That is where hope lies. For just as certain as it is that evil people have used their eloquence to do evil, so also have many Christians been given grace to control their tongues and use whatever eloquence God has given them to teach his Word and praise him both in spirit and in truth.

There will never be genuine tongue control until we possess a new or renewed heart. But that is just what has been given to us when we become Christians. Because of God's renewing work within, we are able to let our "conversation be always full of grace, seasoned with salt" and "know how to answer everyone" wisely and well.

Our Lord's Example

The gracious speech of Jesus is a great example for us, as he is in all other areas. We recall that after the first sermon of his career, spoken in the synagogue at Nazareth, the people were mostly enthralled at his gracious teaching. The text says, "All spoke well of him and were amazed at the gracious words that came from his lips" (Luke 4:22). So it was throughout his three-year ministry.

Here are some examples.

1. His endorsement of John the Baptist.

Matthew tells us in chapter 11 that when he was in prison and doubtless discouraged, John the Baptist sent disciples to Jesus to ask whether he was really the one who was to come or whether

John had been mistaken and should look for another. From some religious leaders a question like that might have provoked harsh words: "Of course, I'm the one. Didn't you get a sign from heaven at the time of my baptism? Don't you believe God? What do you mean asking a question like that at a time like this? Doubt on your part may seriously undermine my credibility!"

Jesus did not say any of those things, of course. Instead, he pointed John to the Scriptures, telling the disciples to report how the blind had been made to see, the lame to walk, and how lepers had been cured, all in line with prophecies such as that in Isaiah 61:1-2, which he had read in the synagogue in Nazareth when he began his ministry. Rather than criticizing John's ministry, Jesus endorsed it, saying,

> What did you go out into the desert to see? A reed
> swayed by the wind? . . . A man dressed in fine
> clothes? No, those who wear fine clothes are in
> kings' palaces. Then what did you go out to see? A
> prophet? Yes, I tell you, and more than a prophet.
> This is the one about whom it is written: "I will
> send my messenger ahead of you, who will prepare
> your way before you." I tell you the truth: Among
> those born of women there has not risen anyone
> greater than John the Baptist. (Matt. 11:7-11)

Those were gracious words indeed.

2. His instruction of Nicodemus.

The third chapter of John recounts Jesus' instruction of Nicodemus when Nicodemus came to him at night to discuss religious matters. Jesus told him that he could not understand them unless he was born again. But instead of sending him away to "get born again," as we might have done, Jesus graciously taught Nicodemus from the Old Testament, since he knew that it is through the teaching of the Word as it is blessed by the Holy Spirit that people are regenerated. Jesus must have taken a rather long time to do this, since the chapter touches on at least eight major doctrines Jesus taught him.

3. His conversation with the Samaritan woman.

The situation was different with the Samaritan woman, whose story is told in John 4. She was no theologian. She knew only the beliefs and prejudices of her people. But Jesus nevertheless led her gently to understand who he was, what he had come to do, and her great need of him. As a result of this gracious conversation, the woman came to trust Jesus as her personal Savior and became a witness to the other people in her town. Later those people had this testimony: "We know that this man really is the Savior of the world" (John 4:42).

4. His concern for the woman who had been caught in adultery.

One day Jesus' enemies brought him a woman who had been caught in the act of committing adultery. Jesus was supposed to condemn her, as required by the law. But he did not. Instead, he demanded that those who were themselves innocent should be the first to cast stones at her. According to the law, the first stones needed to be thrown by those who had borne witness to the crime. But since this was an obvious setup, those persons must have been guilty of what we would call entrapment. They knew it, were convicted of their greater sin, and one by one began to slink away. Then Jesus turned to the woman and forgave her on the basis of his death for sin that was yet to come. "Woman, where are they? Has no one condemned you?" he asked.

"No one, sir," she answered.

"Then neither do I condemn you," Jesus replied. "Go now and leave your life of sin" (John 8:10-11). He forgave her but also taught the necessity of living a holy life. We studied this story at greater length in chapter 3.

5. His restoration of Peter.

My final example is Jesus' gentle restoration of Peter after Peter had denied him at the time of Jesus' arrest and crucifixion. Jesus could have been harsh, humiliating Peter before the others, since Peter had boasted that even if the others denied Jesus, he at least would not. Even then Jesus told Peter that, although he would deny him, Jesus would pray for him so that his faith would not fail, and that when he was restored he would use his experience to strengthen his brothers (Luke 22:31-32). But now, following the Resurrection, Jesus restored Peter both deliberately and gently.

"Simon son of John, do you truly love me more than these?"

Peter remembered his earlier boast and replied without Jesus' pointed comparison to the other disciples, "Yes, Lord, you know that I love you."

Jesus said, "Feed my lambs."

This was repeated three times, corresponding to Peter's three denials (John 21:15-17). It was an exceedingly gracious way of dealing with Peter. It was characteristic of all Jesus said and did.

What Our Conversation Should Be

We may ask again, What should the Christian's conversation be like? What does Colossians 4:6 teach about the way we should use words? There are many things we could say about the way Christians should speak, but this text alone suggests at least five of them.

1. Our words should be kind.

God is kind to us. Therefore, we should be kind when we speak to other people. God's words are gracious words. Ours should be gracious also. This is the first thing Paul indicates when he says that our conversation should be "full of grace."

Is this an apt description of your words? I know a leader in the evangelical church who has a problem at this point. He is a man of unusual gifts and is widely used of the Lord. But he has a way of making hurtful jokes or telling disparaging stories about other people. These stories are not intentionally malicious, as far as I can see. I would assume they arise from his own insecurities. He feels more in charge of things if he can humble someone else. But his words are still unkind and harmful. I have seen people visibly wounded by the things he says.

And they remember it, too. When we were children and other children were making fun of us, as children will, we were taught to say:

> Sticks and stones may break my bones,
> But words will never hurt me.

But it is not true. Words do hurt, and we can all remember harsh things that were said about us or to us, perhaps decades ago.

In his best-selling book *How to Win Friends and Influence People*, the self-taught human relations expert Dale Carnegie tells about something he did as a young man that was very foolish. He was preparing a magazine article about famous American authors and wrote to an author whose name was Richard Harding Davis, asking him about his method of work. A few weeks earlier he had received a letter from someone else. It had been typed by his secretary, and on the bottom there was the notation: "Dictated but not read." Carnegie was impressed. It sounded important. So at the bottom of his letter to Davis, Carnegie added the same phrase: "Dictated but not read."

Davis never even bothered to answer the letter. He simply returned it to Carnegie with these words scribbled across the bottom: "Your bad manners are exceeded only by your bad manners." Carnegie admitted that he had blundered and deserved the rebuke. But he resented the retort and remembered it. He remembered it so vividly that ten years later, when he read in a paper about the death of Richard Harding Davis, the one thing that came to his mind was the hurt Davis had given him.

Words do hurt. Sometimes words kill. So do not harm by your words. "Let your conversation be always full of grace." Speak kindly.

2. Our speech should be serious.

I do not mean by this that Christians should be humorless or grim or always talking about the Bible or theology. We are never told that Jesus laughed, but we know he was witty and that he was an enjoyable person to be with. We do not have to be more serious than Jesus. Yet Jesus was not frivolous either, was he? He never engaged in stupid or mindless conversations. He could enjoy life and have a good time, as he did at the wedding at Cana. But he also knew that what we say is important and that spiritual matters are of the utmost importance. Therefore, when speaking, Jesus always seemed to have the spiritual well-being of other people uppermost in his mind.

I am sure Paul is recommending this in Colossians 4:6 because of the context in which the verse is set. Verse 3: "And pray for us, too, that God may open a door for our message, so that we may proclaim the mystery of Christ, for which I am in chains." Verse 4: "Pray that I may proclaim it clearly, as I should." Verse 5: "Be wise in the way you act toward outsiders; make the most of every opportunity." There is a progression in those verses. *First*, Paul asks prayer for the missionary team that surrounds him: Tychicus (v. 7), Onesimus (v. 9), Aristarchus, Mark, and Barnabas (v. 10), Justus (v. 11), Epaphras (v. 12), Luke and Demas (v. 14). *Second*, he asks prayer for himself, that he might be a good witness. *Third,* he encourages the believers at Colosse to make the most of every opportunity, undoubtedly referring to their own opportunities to share the gospel. It is immediately after this that he says, "Let your conversation be always full of grace."

In developing the previous point I have assumed that "full of grace" means "gracious." But in view of this context, it might equally well mean "full of the doctrines of the grace of God." That is, "Let a lot of what you talk about be God's grace."

Is your conversation serious in this sense? Do you talk about spiritual things often? Are you considering the spiritual need of other people as you do? At the end of the Old Testament we are told that the godly in Malachi's day did this: "Then those who feared the LORD talked with each other, and the LORD listened and heard." They were talking about spiritual things. Then we are told, "A scroll of remembrance was written in [God's] presence concerning those who feared the LORD and honored his name" (Mal. 3:16).

Job wanted his words to count. He said, "Oh, that my words were recorded, that they were written on a scroll, that they were inscribed with an iron tool on lead, or engraved in rock forever!" (Job 19:23-24).

Paul wrote to Titus recommending "soundness of speech that cannot be condemned" (Titus 2:8).

3. Our comments should be discerning.

This is what Paul is speaking about when he tells us to "make the most of every opportunity." Not every moment of our day contains opportunities for sharing the gospel or speaking a timely or encouraging word. In fact, some moments are decidedly inopportune. If people in your company are rushing to satisfy a customer by meeting a critical deadline, that is not the time to distract them by opening a serious discussion about sin.

If you are asked to honor an employee who is retiring after thirty years of good service, that is not the time to ask, "By the way, do all of you know the four spiritual laws?" That would be inappropriate, unwise, and offensive.

On the other hand, there are many more opportunities to speak about things that matter than most of us are conscious of, and a discerning person will pick up on them. People betray their anxieties in countless small ways, and a discerning Christian will quickly relate to these and testify to the peace and contentment that faith in Jesus brings. Discussion of current events can turn to the root causes lying beneath the world's problems. The collapse of national morality can lead to a discussion of the need for inner spiritual change, which only God can give.

Also, we can create opportunities. Paul Little tells how he would often ask another person: "Are you a Christian, or are you still on the way?" That presented an easy alternative, and if they were not sure and said that they were still on the way, he would follow with: "How far along the way are you?" Many serious, helpful, and inoffensive conversations followed.

4. Our statements should be wise.

We all know the story of the zealous Christian barber who wanted to witness to his customers. So when he had them in the chair, had lathered their face, and was about to shave them with a large straight razor, he would ask quite suddenly and fiercely: "Are you ready to die?" He could never understand why some immediately bolted from the chair and never came back. His witnessing was zealous, but it was unwise. Paul says in Colossians 4 that our conversation should always be wise, prefacing verse 6 with the words, "Be wise in the way you act toward outsiders," and ending his words about our conversations with the clause, "so that you may know how to answer everyone."

How to speak, when to speak, and when not to speak are all

matters that involve wisdom. But when we think of our conversations being wise, we should also think of the content of what we say and how true wisdom is found not in the world's insights but in the Bible. In its darkened and sinful state the world may not regard this as wisdom. Paul says that when he preached the gospel the Greeks regarded it as foolishness. Nevertheless, the things of God are true wisdom, and we should be known as those who believe and often repeat these wise words. Paul told the Corinthians, "The foolishness of God is wiser than man's wisdom, and the weakness of God is stronger than man's strength" (1 Cor. 1:25).

True wisdom comes from God through the instruction in the Bible, and the conversations of Christians should be filled with it.

5. Our conversation should be interesting.

My final point is that the conversation of Christians should be interesting, which is the way I understand the phrase "seasoned with salt." Salt had various uses in the ancient world, the chief one being that it was used as a preservative. There was no refrigeration then, of course. So if meat was to be preserved, for instance, the only way of doing it was by smoking it or curing it with salt. Jesus was probably thinking about this use of salt when he told his disciples that they were "the salt of the earth" (Matt. 5:13). He meant that it is due to the influence of godly people that the world is not a more rotten place than it is.

But that is not what Paul is thinking of in this verse from Colossians, for here he uses the words "seasoned with." This is not referring to salt's preservative powers but to salt's ability to contribute flavor to something that might otherwise be insipid.

Is your conversation like that? Is it interesting? I am afraid that many Christians are dull in what they say because they are not thinking much about important matters and can only comment on the latest sports scores or the weather. Yet it is also true that the most interesting of all people are Christians, in my judgment, particularly if they are studying God's Word and learning to think about life as Christians. People like this do not merely reflect the warmed-over views or hackneyed clichés of the gray, dull world around them. Their minds are alive with new ideas, and their conversation is provocative and intriguing.

Throughout the year my speaking schedule brings me into contact with many such people. I am always stimulated by these contacts. Shouldn't your speech be lively? Shouldn't your conversation be at least as well prepared, satisfying, and tasty as the conversation between Neil Postman and Camille Paglia that I referred to in the introduction to this study?

A Few Important Warnings

There is one more matter before I end. I have written about what our speech should be, but I also want to note that there are important biblical warnings about what our words should not be.

First, they should not be *arrogant*, that is, pretending to have answers to questions we do not actually have. Remember Job's counselors. God called their words "words without knowledge" (Job 38:2), and Job rightly complained that their ignorant counsel harmed him. He asked his friends, "How long will you torment me and crush me with words?" (Job 19:2).

Second, our words should not be *divisive*. Some people think that in order to defend truth they have to be argumentative. But Paul warned Timothy about godless men whose arguments "result in envy, strife, malicious talk, evil suspicions and constant friction between men of corrupt mind" (1 Tim. 6:4-5). He also said, "Warn [Christians] before God against quarreling about words" (2 Tim. 2:14).

Third, our words should not be *careless*. Remember Jesus' warning about the place words will have in the final judgment. He said, "Men will have to give account on the day of judgment for every careless word they have spoken. For by your words you will be acquitted, and by your words you will be condemned" (Matt. 12:36-37).

Words are important! Your conversation counts!

"May the words of my mouth and the meditation of my heart be pleasing in your sight, O LORD, my Rock and my Redeemer" (Ps. 19:14).

Part Four

GRACE TRIUMPHANT

Chapter 16

PERSEVERING GRACE

And the God of all grace, who called you to his eternal
glory in Christ, after you have suffered a little
while, will himself restore you and make you strong,
firm and steadfast. 1 PETER 5:10

You may recall from chapter 1 that we began looking at the subject of grace by listing the many adjectives linked to grace in Christian theology and hymnody.

In the back of the *Trinity Hymnal*, the hymnbook we use in our church, the following categories for grace are listed: converting grace, the covenant of grace, efficacious grace, the fullness of grace, magnified grace, refreshing grace, regenerating grace, sanctifying grace, saving grace, and sovereign grace (as well as such combined listings as the love and grace of God, the love and grace of Christ, the love and grace of the Holy Spirit, and salvation by grace). The hymns themselves use words like *abounding grace, abundant grace, amazing grace, boundless grace, fountain of grace, God of grace, indelible grace, marvelous grace, matchless grace, overflowing grace, pardoning grace, plenteous grace, unfailing grace, unmeasurable grace, wondrous grace, the word of grace, grace all sufficient,* and *grace alone.*

Theologians add to the list by speaking of *common grace, electing grace, irresistible grace, persevering grace, prevenient grace,* and *pursuing grace.*

In this study we come to one of those theological phrases: *persevering grace.* It means that God will persevere with those whom he has called to faith in Christ so that none will be lost and that, because he perseveres with them, they also will persevere, resisting and overcoming the world, the flesh, and the devil, and thus being ready for Jesus when he comes for them. But in turning to this phrase, there is a sense in which we are actually only summing up the other phrases. For when we say that God perseveres with us by grace or according to his gracious nature, we are also saying that he has chosen us by his electing grace, has called us by his irresistible grace, has blessed us with his abounding grace, is sanctifying us by his efficacious grace, is unfailing in his persevering grace, and will eventually bring us through the trials of this life to heaven—and that this is by his amazing grace alone.

Or to put the doctrine in other words, persevering grace means that God never begins a work he does not graciously bring to full completion. He is the Omega as well as the Alpha, the beginning *and* the end of all things.

This reminds us of Philippians 1:6, one of the three greatest verses or sections of the Bible having to do with perseverance: "Being confident of this, that he who began a good work in you will carry it on to completion until the day of Christ Jesus."

The two other outstanding passages are in John and Romans:

> My sheep listen to my voice; I know them, and
> they follow me. I give them eternal life, and they
> shall never perish; no one can snatch them out of

my hand. My Father, who has given them to me, is greater than all; no one can snatch them out of my Father's hand. I and the Father are one. (John 10:27-30)

Who shall separate us from the love of Christ? Shall trouble or hardship or persecution or famine or nakedness or danger or sword? As it is written: "For your sake we face death all day long; we are considered as sheep to be slaughtered." No, in all these things we are more than conquerors through him who loved us. For I am convinced that neither death nor life, neither angels nor demons, neither the present nor the future, nor any powers, neither height nor depth, nor anything else in all creation, will be able to separate us from the love of God that is in Christ Jesus our Lord. (Rom. 8:35-39)

Another Perseverance Promise

Yet these are not the only verses in the Bible that teach perseverance, and it is actually to another one that we turn now because of its use of the word *grace*: "And the God of all grace, who called you to his eternal glory in Christ, after you have suffered a little while, will himself restore you and make you strong, firm and steadfast" (1 Pet. 5:10).

Here are a few important things to know before we begin to examine this verse in detail.

1. First Peter was written to Christians scattered throughout certain areas of Asia Minor, modern-day Turkey.

Peter calls these people "God's elect, strangers in the world" (1 Pet. 1:1).

2. These believers had been suffering many kinds of trials.

There are four references to their trials in the letter (see 1 Pet. 1:6-7; 3:13-17; 4:12-19; and 5:9). These references indicate that the suffering the Christians were experiencing included malicious slander from unbelievers, possible persecution from government authorities, and spiritual assaults from Satan.

3. Peter wanted to encourage them by the certainty of the coming glory.

He does this throughout the letter. In chapter 1 he speaks of the believers' "living hope" (v. 3) and of "an inheritance that can never perish, spoil or fade—kept in heaven for you" (v. 4). He says that their trials have come so that their "faith—of greater worth than gold, which perishes even though refined by fire—may be proved genuine and may result in praise, glory and honor when Jesus Christ is revealed" (v. 7). In chapter 3 he reminds them that "Christ died for sins once for all, the righteous for the unrighteous, to bring you to God" (v. 18). In chapter 4 he says, "Rejoice that you participate in the sufferings of Christ, so that you may be overjoyed when his glory is revealed" (v. 13).

This is what the text we are studying also does. It encourages the Christians of Asia Minor by reminding them of the glory that is to be theirs when they complete their earthly course and are with the Lord Jesus Christ in heaven, and it assures them that in the meantime God will strengthen them and keep them for the work they have to do here.

The text is a benediction, that is, a word of blessing. But it is important to note that the verbs in the verse are future, not optative. That is, they express a promise, not a wish. If it were the latter, the verse would say something like: "May the God of all grace . . . restore you and make you strong." Benedictions are often like that, and this is the way the King James Version actually translates Peter's words: "The God of all grace . . . make you perfect, stablish, strengthen, settle you." But the verse is actually a promise in the future tense, not a wish, and what it promises is that "the God of all grace, who called you to his eternal glory in Christ, after you have suffered a little while, *will* himself *restore you and make you strong, firm and steadfast.*"

It is this future tense that makes 1 Peter 5:10 an important verse about perseverance.

No Escape from Suffering

The first truth we see when we turn to this text is that perseverance does not mean that believers in Christ are automatically delivered from all suffering. In fact, the verse teaches the opposite. It teaches that we will experience suffering, though it will be of relatively short duration (for this life rather than for eternity) and that suffering will be replaced in time by an eternal glory.

Where did Peter get this understanding of suffering in the Christian life? It is no great mystery. He learned it from Jesus Christ. This was one of the themes of the last discourses of Jesus before his crucifixion, recorded in chapters 14-16 of John's Gospel. In chapter 15 Jesus spoke of the world's hatred, which would lead to persecutions: "If the world hates you, keep in mind that it hated me first. If you belonged to the world, it would love you as its own. As it is, you do not belong to the world, but I have chosen you out of the world. That is why the world hates you. . . . If they persecuted me, they will persecute you also" (vv. 18-20). In the next chapter he tells of religious persecutions: "They will put you out of the synagogue; in fact, a time is coming when anyone who kills you will think he is offering a service to God. They will do such things because they have not known the Father or me" (vv. 2-3). His final words in the discourse were: "In this world you will have trouble. But take heart! I have overcome the world" (v. 33).

Obviously, Peter had learned from this. His personal experiences as a Christian as well as his observations of the life and experiences of the early Christian community assured him that Jesus was not being hypothetical when he forecast suffering and persecution for his followers. Suffering is a very real thing.

You will also notice something else important if you glance back one or two verses and place verse 10 in that context. In verses 8 and 9 Peter is talking about Satan, the devil, and he is saying that the suffering he is concerned about here is the suffering Satan causes. He calls Satan the Christian's enemy. "Your enemy the devil prowls around like a roaring lion looking for someone to devour. Resist him, standing firm in the faith, because you know that your brothers throughout the world are undergoing the same kind of sufferings."

There are many names for the devil in the Bible. *Devil* itself is one; it means "disrupter" or "destroyer of peace." *Satan* means "accuser"; we are told in Revelation that Satan, "the accuser of our brothers, . . . accuses them before our God day and night" (Rev. 12:10). Satan is called *Belial*, meaning "something low or morally depraved." He is called "the tempter," "the god and prince of this world," the "chief of demons," *Beelzebub* (meaning "Lord of the flies"), *Apollyon*, a "murderer from the beginning," and "the great dragon . . . that ancient serpent called the devil." In our text he is compared to a "lion looking for someone to devour." A lion is a fierce and powerful animal and a subtle stalker of prey. So when Peter warns us about our enemy the lion, he is assuring us that however wonderful the doctrine of perseverance is, it does not mean that we shall be spared Satan's onslaughts and that, in fact, we had better be prepared to resist him and so stand firm in the faith to which we have been called.

But how can we do that if Satan is really as powerful as the

Bible says he is? The answer, of course, is that in ourselves we cannot resist him even for a moment. We can only do it by the grace and power of God, which is where our text comes in. For it assures us that in spite of these satanic threats to our security, "the God of grace, who called you to his eternal glory in Christ . . . will himself restore you and make you strong, firm and steadfast."

Peter had learned this from Jesus, too. You will recall how Jesus told Peter at the Last Supper that "Satan has asked to sift you as wheat" (Luke 22:31). The devil must have meant, "I know you are placing a lot of hope in these twelve disciples that you will be leaving behind when you return to heaven. But it is a hopeless gamble, and I will show you how hopeless it really is. If you will just let me get at Peter, your leading apostle, I will shake him so badly that all his faith will come tumbling out like chaff at threshing time, and he will be utterly ruined." Satan is a liar, but I do not think he was lying at this point. He must have remembered how easy it had been for him to ruin our first parents in Eden long ago, and he concluded that if he had brought Adam and Eve to ruin when they were in their unfallen and pristine glory, it should have been easy to knock down Peter, who was (unlike Adam) already sinful, ignorant, brash, and ridiculously self-confident.

And he was right. Peter had boasted that he would never deny Jesus. He said, "Lord, I am ready to go with you to prison and to death" (v. 33). But when Satan blew upon him he fell. In fact, it took only a little servant girl to say of Peter, "This man was with him [that is, with Jesus]" (v. 56), and immediately Peter denied that he even knew the Lord.

Yet what Satan had not counted on was what Jesus also told Peter in the upper room. He warned him that Satan would indeed attack him and that he would fall, but he added, "I have prayed for you, Simon, that your faith may not fail. And when you have turned back, strengthen your brothers" (v. 32). If Peter could explain that statement to us, he would probably say something like this: "When Jesus told me he had prayed for me so that my faith would not fail, he was telling me that I could not stand against Satan alone. And neither can you! Satan is much too powerful for us. So do not make the mistake I made, assuming that because I loved Jesus I could never be led by Satan to deny that I ever knew him. Satan can bend us any way he wishes. But if we are joined to Jesus, we will find that he is able to keep us from falling, or if he allows us to fall, he is able to keep us from falling the whole way and will in any case forgive us, bring us back to himself, and give us meaningful work to do."

Some years ago I heard Professor John Gerstner reflect on this story, claiming (in jest) that before his fall Peter had written a hymn that is not in the hymnbook I use but which I have occasionally heard sung. It goes, "Lord, we are able. . . ." But what Peter learned is that we are *not* able, not in ourselves, and that if we are to stand against Satan, it must be by the persevering grace of God, who has promised to restore us and make us strong, firm, and steadfast.

Four Things God Will Do

In one respect, the King James translation of 1 Peter 5:10 is not as accurate as the New International Version, because it turns the promise "God . . . will . . . restore you" into a wish: "The God of all grace . . . make you perfect, stablish, strengthen, settle you." I mentioned that matter earlier. However, there is one way in which the King James Version is closer to the Greek text than the New International Version, and this is the way in which it lists the four things Peter says God will do for believers. For some reason the New International Version breaks them up, saying that God "will himself restore you and make you strong, firm and steadfast." But in the original text these are merely four powerful verbs, each in the future tense: "will perfect," "will establish," "will strengthen" and "will settle." There are no additional words. In other words, the verse simply lists four things that God will do for all believers.

1. God will perfect you.

The word the King James Version translated "perfect" means "to make fully ready" or "to complete." It was used of making fishing nets ready by mending them, which is probably where the New International Version translators got the idea of restoration. Or perhaps they were thinking of Peter's experience of having denied Jesus and of later being restored. But it is not really this that Peter is thinking of. He has spoken of suffering, and the idea is not that we are restored from suffering but rather that suffering is used by God to complete or perfect what he is doing with us.

The same idea emerges if we think of grace. The verse begins "and the God of all grace," which means that God is the source of every grace and will supply what we need to go on to spiritual wholeness or perfection. Earlier I listed the graces of electing, calling, sanctifying, and so on. At this point, in view of our being attacked by Satan, it might be more helpful to think of the Christian's armor, which God also graciously supplies.

Paul lists the articles of a Christian's armor in Ephesians 6, making some of the same points Peter is making in his letter:

> Finally, be strong in the Lord and in his mighty
> power. Put on the full armor of God so that you
> can take your stand against the devil's schemes. . . .
> Stand firm then, with the belt of truth buckled
> around your waist, with the breastplate of righ-
> teousness in place, and with your feet fitted with

the readiness that comes from the gospel of peace.
In addition to all this, take up the shield of faith,
with which you can extinguish all the flaming
arrows of the evil one. Take the helmet of salvation
and the sword of the Spirit, which is the word of
God. (Eph. 6:10-11, 14-17)

2. God will establish you.

The idea conveyed by this verb is to be established in a firm, defensive position so that the attacks of the devil will not dislodge the Christian from it. The one who is established will be able to hold his or her ground.

If you and I have any understanding of ourselves, we must at times worry greatly about being dislodged from where God has placed us. We know how weak we are and how fierce an antagonist Satan is. What if Satan should attack our home? Can my husband and I really hold it together? What if he attacks our children? Our marriage itself? Suppose I lose my job? Or my health? What about my Christian witness? Suppose the people I work with ostracize me because of my Christian faith, make fun of me, shut me out of office confidences, or pass over me for promotions? Will I really be able to stand firm under such pressures? Or will I be ashamed of Jesus and disgrace him by refusing to speak up for him or by compromising what I stand for? What if I should even deny him, as Peter did?

Those fears are not groundless, because we know that Christian homes sometimes are broken up, that Christians often fail to stand for Christ, and that some do occasionally deny him. In the midst of our fears this text comes as a great promise. "God will establish you." He will keep you through just such pressured situations. And if, in accord with his own wise counsel, he should allow you to stumble for a time and fall, you can know that Jesus has nevertheless prayed for you and that your fall will not be permanent. In fact, when it is past you will be stronger than you were before, and you will be able to use your experience of the grace of God to help others.

3. God will strengthen you.

The previous promise, that "God will establish you," had to do with holding one's ground. That is, it concerned a defensive stand. This promise goes further. It concerns an offensive action. It says that God will "strengthen" us to resist Satan, which is exactly what Peter told us to do in the previous verse: "Resist him, standing firm in the faith, because you know that your brothers throughout the world are undergoing the same kind of sufferings" (v. 9). We cannot resist Satan in our own strength, but we can if God strengthens us.

4. God will settle you.

The last of these four promises is that God will "settle" us. The word means "to be made to rest securely," like a strong building on a sure foundation. It is important for this reason. The purpose of the attacks of Satan is to dislodge us from our foundation, which is Jesus Christ. He will do that if he can. God's purpose is to settle us in or on Jesus, and God has arranged things so that the attacks of Satan, rather than unsettling us, actually serve to bond us to that foundation even more firmly than before. That is why Paul told the Romans, "We also rejoice in our sufferings, because we know that suffering produces perseverance; perseverance, character; and character, hope" (Rom. 5:3-4).

That happened to Peter himself. Before he was tempted by Satan, Peter thought he was secure, but he was not because he was trusting in himself. After he had been tempted, he knew that he could never prevail against Satan in his own strength and therefore stayed close to Jesus. It was from that proximity to Jesus and by resting on that foundation that Peter was able to strengthen his brethren in like situations, which is what Jesus said he would do and what he is actually doing here.

We have a natural tendency to rely upon ourselves. But God has arranged even the assaults of Satan so that we will be weaned away from self-reliance to trust God instead. Few experiences in life are more useful in settling us on the only sure foundation than the temptations and sufferings that come to us from Satan.

Grace and Glory

Earlier I spoke of the glory that is mentioned in this verse as the Christian's ultimate destiny and sure hope: "God, who called you to his eternal glory in Christ. . . ." Glory is the obvious place to end a study of the subject of the persevering grace of God. Grace perseveres with us precisely so that we might be brought to glory.

But glory is a difficult term to define. The Hebrew language has two words for it: *kabod*, which has the idea of "weight," therefore of that which has value; and *shekinah*, which refers to the unapproachable light that surrounds and represents the Deity. In the New Testament the word for glory is *doxa*, which is used to translate both Hebrew words and embraces both of the Hebrew ideas. All three words are chiefly used of God, as in Psalm 24, which describes God as the King of glory.

> Lift up your heads, O you gates; lift them up, you
> ancient doors, that the King of glory may come in.
> Who is he, this King of glory? The LORD Al-
> mighty—he is the King of glory. (Ps. 24:9-10)

The psalm is teaching that God alone is of ultimate weight, worth, or value, and because of that, he only is worthy of our highest praise.

The problem with understanding *glory* comes when we realize that the word is also used in connection with our destiny, as in 1 Peter 5. Peter speaks of our being "called . . . to his eternal glory." What does that mean? It could mean merely being called to God himself, that is, to God's presence. But when we look at other relevant Bible passages we see that it means more than this. It means that we shall also share in God's glory, that we shall be glorified. In other words, it does not refer only to where we will end up as Christians, but also to what we will be and how we will be received when we get there.

In my judgment the most stimulating thing that has been written on glory is an essay by C. S. Lewis, titled "The Weight of Glory." Quite possibly it is the best thing this brilliant English scholar and Christian apologist ever wrote. Lewis begins by admitting that for many years the idea of glory seemed unattractive to him because he associated it only with fame or luminosity. The first idea seemed wicked. Why should we want to be famous? Isn't that un-Christian? And as for the second, well, who wants to go around looking like a high-powered electric light bulb?

However, as he looked into the matter, Lewis discovered that wanting to receive God's approval was not at all wicked. He remembered how Jesus said that no one can enter heaven except as a child, and he reflected on how natural and proper it is for a child to be pleased when he or she is praised. There is a wrong way of desiring praise, of course. It occurs when we want praise to come to us rather than to someone else. Moreover, it is always easy for a right desire for praise to slip over into a warped and evil desire and so be harmful. But pursued in the right way, pleasure at being praised is the exact opposite of the pride Lewis had at first thought it signified. It is actually humility of a childlike sort. Since God is our Father, it is right that we should want to please him and be pleased at having pleased him.

This is not due to anything in ourselves. Salvation is God's work from start to finish. But what Lewis is saying is that for Christians the day will come when we will stand before God, he having persevered with us until the end, and then he shall look upon us and be pleased with what he sees. He will say when he looks at us, "It has all been worthwhile. It was good for me to have sent my Son to die on that cross, suffering the pain, agony, and torment of the crucifixion to save this sinner from his sins. He is what I wanted to make him. He is like my Son. I am satisfied. I am very well pleased." When we hear that, we will be well pleased, too. And, far from taking glory to ourselves for what has happened, we will glorify him who has in that way glorified us.

Lewis says that the opposite of glory is to be ignored by God, to be rejected, exiled, and estranged. To be glorified is to be noticed, welcomed, received, acknowledged, and let in.

He has this encouragement, too:

> If we take the imagery of Scripture seriously, if we believe that God will one day give us the Morning Star and cause us to *put on* the splendor of the sun, then we may surmise that both the ancient myths and the modern poetry, so false as history, may be very near the truth as prophecy. At present we are on the outside of the world, the wrong side of the door. We discern the freshness and purity of the morning, but they do not make us fresh and pure. We cannot mingle with the splendors we see. But all the leaves of the New Testament are rustling with the rumor that it will not always be so. Some day, God willing, we shall get in. When human souls have become as perfect in voluntary obedience as the inanimate creation is in its lifeless obedience, then they will put on its glory, or rather that greater glory of which Nature is only the first sketch.

Lewis was a professor of literature, not a theologian, and he freely admits that much of what he has written about glory in his essay is human speculation. But he has captured something of the wonder of what is in store for those who have become the objects of the electing, sanctifying, and persevering grace of God. Isn't it splendid? And shouldn't it transform how we look at the experiences we are passing through now?

The English hymn writer W. H. Burleigh thought so. He wrote:

> Let us press on, in patient self-denial,
> Accept the hardship, shrink not from the loss;
> Our portion lies beyond the hour of trial,
> Our crown beyond the cross.

Chapter 17

GRACE BE WITH YOU ALL

The grace of the Lord Jesus be with God's people.
Amen. REVELATION 22:21

We have come to the end of a study of one of the most wonderful ideas in the Bible, the doctrine of God's amazing grace. And we have also come to the very last verse of the Bible, which not surprisingly is about grace also. In the first chapter of these studies we began with Genesis. Now we end with the very last verse of Revelation.

The verse is a benediction. *Benediction* literally means "to speak a good word concerning somebody" or "to wish another well." In biblical language specifically it is a wish that God might be gracious to or bless another person. In the last chapter we were looking at a verse that sounds like a benediction but is actually a promise: "And the God of all grace, who called you to his eternal glory in Christ, after you have suffered a little while, will himself restore you and make you strong, firm and steadfast" (1 Pet. 5:10). That verse tells us what God will do. The last verse in the Bible, the verse we are going to consider now, is a true benediction. It is the wish or fervent desire that "the grace of the Lord Jesus Christ [might] be with God's people."

Many "Grace" Benedictions

I have not taken the time to count the Bible's benedictions, but it is no exaggeration to say that there must be hundreds of them. There are even scores that contain the word *grace*, the subject of these studies.

I noticed that fact early in my preparation for this series. So when I began the series of sermons, which have become the chapters of this book, I decided to end each of the worship services with a different benediction that included the word *grace*. I did that in nearly every case for a period of four or five months. Here are some of these splendid benedictions.

> Grace and peace to you from God our Father and from the Lord Jesus Christ. (Rom. 1:7)

> The grace of our Lord Jesus be with you. (Rom. 16:20)

> Grace and peace to you from God our Father and the Lord Jesus Christ. (1 Cor. 1:3)

> The grace of the Lord Jesus be with you. (1 Cor. 16:23)

> Grace and peace to you from God our Father and the Lord Jesus Christ. (2 Cor. 1:2)

> May the grace of the Lord Jesus Christ, and the love of God, and the fellowship of the Holy Spirit be with you all. (2 Cor. 13:14)

> Grace and peace to you from God our Father and the Lord Jesus Christ. (Eph. 1:2)

Grace to all who love our Lord Jesus Christ with an undying love. (Eph. 6:24)

Grace and peace to you from God our Father and the Lord Jesus Christ. (Phil. 1:2)

The grace of the Lord Jesus Christ be with your spirit. Amen. (Phil. 4:23)

Grace and peace to you from God our Father. (Col. 1:2)

Grace be with you. (Col. 4:18)

Grace and peace to you. (1 Thess. 1:1)

The grace of our Lord Jesus Christ be with you. (1 Thess. 5:28)

Grace and peace to you. (2 Thess. 1:2)

The grace of our Lord Jesus Christ be with you all. (2 Thess. 3:18)

Grace, mercy and peace from God the Father and Christ Jesus our Lord. (1 Tim. 1:2)

Grace be with you. (1 Tim. 6:21)

Grace, mercy and peace from God the Father and Christ Jesus our Lord. (2 Tim. 1:2)

The Lord be with your spirit. Grace be with you. (2 Tim. 4:22)

Grace and peace from God the Father and Christ Jesus our Savior. (Titus 1:4)

Grace be with you all. (Titus 3:15)

The grace of the Lord Jesus Christ be with your spirit. (Philem. 25)

Grace be with you all. (Heb. 13:25)

Grace and peace be yours in abundance. (1 Pet. 1:2)

Grace and peace be yours in abundance through the knowledge of God and of Jesus our Lord. (2 Pet. 1:2)

Grace and peace to you from him who is, and who was, and who is to come. (Rev. 1:4)

And the last one, our text:

The grace of the Lord Jesus be with God's people. Amen. (Rev. 22:21)

These benedictions are most frequent in Paul's letters, but they are scattered throughout the New Testament and are abundant, several of them even appearing in a single book or letter. Frequently grace is linked with two other blessings that we have also received from God: mercy and peace. These are said to have come to us from God the Father and from or through the Lord Jesus Christ. Although the words appear in different combinations, the most complete form of these benedictions is the one found in 2 Corinthians 13:14: "May the grace of the Lord Jesus Christ, and the love of God, and the fellowship of the Holy Spirit be with you all."

The Grace of the Lord Jesus Christ

Revelation 22:21 does not contain all the elements of the more complete benedictions, but it is in line with them when it links the blessing of grace explicitly to Jesus Christ. In the early chapters of this series we saw that although grace is known in the Old Testament, there is a sense in which it only became fully known with the coming of Jesus. Paul told Timothy, "This grace was given us in Christ Jesus before the beginning of time, but it has now been revealed through the appearing of our Savior, Christ Jesus, who has destroyed death and has brought life and immortality to light through the gospel" (2 Tim. 1:9-10).

John 1:17 expressed this same truth simply, saying, "The law was given through Moses; grace and truth came through Jesus Christ."

As mentioned earlier, in the New International Version there are only eight uses of the word *grace* in the Old Testament, but there are 128 uses of *grace* in the New Testament. In some cases the word occurs several times in a single passage or chapter, as in the important chapter Romans 5. *Grace* occurs seven times in the last half of Romans 5 alone. The word also occurs extensively in Ephesians 1 and 2 and other passages.

There are other Old Testament words for grace, of course.

Gracious is found 39 times in the Old Testament (NIV), seven times as an exact or near repetition of Exodus 34:6, "The LORD, the LORD, the compassionate and gracious God, slow to anger, abounding in love and faithfulness, maintaining love to thousands, forgiving wickedness, rebellion and sin" (cf. Neh. 9:17; Pss. 86:15; 103:8; 145:8; Joel 2:13; Jonah 4:2). That text is important because it tells us that it is God's very nature to be gracious. In the same way, *favor* is used 98 times in the Old Testament, though many of these are of human favor only.

So there really is a difference between the Old Testament and the New Testament at this point, and John was not overstating the matter when he wrote of grace coming in a special way with Jesus. It is significant that it is this same author, John the beloved disciple, who ends his final book and thus also the entire Bible with the words "The grace of the Lord Jesus be with God's people. Amen."

The New Testament associates grace with the Lord Jesus Christ especially, because it is through his death and by his resurrection that sinful men and women have been made righteous before God.

Doctrines of Grace

Another way of showing how closely grace is associated with the person and work of Jesus Christ is by reviewing what in theology are often called "the doctrines of grace," that is, those core doctrines that emphasize the totality of God's sovereign grace in salvation matters. These doctrines are usually presented under the acrostic of the TULIP, where *T* stands for "total depravity," *U* for "unconditional election," *L* for "limited atonement," *I* for "irresistible grace," and *P* for the "perseverance of the saints." Those are not the best of all phrases for describing what is meant by the doctrines of grace, but the truths themselves are at the heart of what is involved in salvation and stress how it is entirely of God.

1. Total depravity.

The first of these doctrines is not an expression of grace itself so much as an explanation of why the grace of God is so necessary. Total depravity means that we are unable to do anything to help ourselves, unable even to respond to the preaching of the gospel when we hear it unless God first works in us to make our response possible. The doctrine is better expressed as "radical depravity," meaning that evil lies at the center of our fallen natures and that it affects every part of our being.

The importance of the first doctrine of grace is that it is our depravity that makes "the grace of the Lord Jesus Christ" necessary.

2. Unconditional election.

These words mean that the determining factor in our salvation is not our choice of God but rather his choice of us and that he chose us long before we even knew of him, in fact, before we were even created or anything was created. The Bible teaches that in that time before time, when only God existed, God determined to create a race of human beings who would fall into sin and come under his wrath through the disobedience of their first parents, and that God determined to save a specific number of them by the work of the Lord Jesus Christ, who would die for them.

And here is the interesting thing. The Bible says that God "chose us in him [that is, in Jesus Christ] before the creation of the world" (Eph. 1:4). In other words, God's electing grace was not exercised apart from Jesus. If the doctrine of total depravity means that "the grace of the Lord Jesus Christ" is necessary if we are to be saved, then the doctrine of unconditional election means that it is only in Jesus that we have this election.

3. Limited atonement.

This is a terrible phrase for describing what is meant by this point of the TULIP, for the intent is not to limit the value of the atoning work of Jesus but rather to show that it is efficacious in the sense that it actually saves those for whom Jesus specifically came to die. It would be much better to call this "definite atonement" or "particular redemption," as reformed people to-day generally do. It means that Jesus' death did not merely make salvation possible for people; he actually saved those for whom he died. He did not merely make redemption possible; he redeemed those whom the Father had given him from before the creation of the world. He did not merely make reconciliation between God and sinners possible; he actually reconciled the elect to God, "making peace through his blood" (Col. 1:20). To use still another term, the death of Jesus Christ secured their justification (Rom. 5:9).

Since Jesus' atonement stands at the center of the work of

God in saving us from sin, we can say that it alone procures "the grace of the Lord Jesus Christ" for us or makes grace possible.

4. Irresistible grace.

This phrase refers to the way God calls us to faith in Jesus Christ. Or rather, it is the Holy Spirit or the Spirit of Jesus who calls. Left to ourselves, we might hear the call in a superficial manner. That is, we might understand the gospel intellectually. But we would certainly reject it. However, when the Spirit of Jesus calls, we are awakened to spiritual life from spiritual death and are thus irresistibly drawn to believe on and follow after Jesus. A good way of expressing this is to say that the Holy Spirit regenerates us, giving us a new nature, as a result of which we do what the new nature naturally does, which is to believe the gospel and trust Christ.

Irresistible grace means that Jesus calls us effectively. Without this "grace of the Lord Jesus Christ" we would reject him.

5. Perseverance of the saints.

The final grace doctrine is the one we explored in the last chapter: perseverance. It has two aspects. On the one hand, it means that the redeemed will persevere in faith until the very end, when Jesus returns for them or they die. On the other hand, it means that the only reason they are able to do this is because God, for his part, also perseveres with them. First Peter 5:10 expressed this by promising that "the God of all grace, who called you to his eternal glory in Christ, after you have suffered a little while, will himself restore you and make you strong, firm and steadfast."

Even this is a "grace of the Lord Jesus Christ." As we saw in the case of Peter's failure in denying that he knew Jesus, it was only because Jesus prayed for Peter that Peter's denial did not cause him to fall away completely, but instead became an experience that strengthened his faith and enabled him later to strengthen others.

So there is every reason why the Bible ends by emphasizing "the grace of the Lord Jesus Christ" specifically. It is because we have been chosen in him before the creation of the world, saved by his death for us in time, called to faith by the Holy Spirit of Christ, and are being preserved in this life by his prayers for us and by his favor.

Growth in Grace

But the verse that ends the Bible is also a wish, as I wrote earlier. It is a wish that "the grace of the Lord Jesus Christ [might] be with God's people." How are we to understand this? Thus far nearly everything I have said about grace has been in the past tense, meaning that God has revealed his grace to us or has been gracious to us in Christ Jesus. Or else it has been a promise that God will continue to be gracious. How is it, then, that we can wish the grace of the Lord Jesus Christ to be with anybody?

Revelation 22:21 does not tell us itself, but by thinking of other Bible verses about grace, we can notice that there are at least four ways this can and should be done.

1. We need to be settled in the great grace doctrines.

Therefore, we can pray that those who know Jesus Christ as Savior might be so settled. There seem to be several ways we can fail to be settled in grace. For one thing, we fail to be settled whenever we allow something other than Jesus Christ to be at the center of our lives. The prophet Jonah learned this through trying to put his own plans ahead of what God had called him to do. His conclusion: "Those who cling to worthless idols forfeit the grace that could be theirs" (Jon. 2:8). Another way we can fail to be settled in the grace of God is when we forget how gracious God has been to us and therefore become harsh with others. The author of Hebrews seems to have this in mind when he writes, "See to it that no one misses the grace of God and that no bitter root grows up to cause trouble and defile many" (Heb. 12:15). Hebrews also refers to a third way this can happen. It is by substituting the mere form of Christianity for the gospel. Therefore, he says, "It is good for our hearts to be strengthened by grace, not by ceremonial foods" (Heb. 13:9).

The cure for these multifaceted ills is to be so aware of the nature of the grace of God in saving us that we become enamored of Jesus Christ and never forget that it is by grace alone that we have been brought out of death and darkness into God's marvelous life and light.

2. We need to grow in the knowledge of God's grace.

Knowledge of the grace of God is not a static thing. Nothing in human life is. Therefore, we need to ask God that those we are concerned for might continually grow in that knowledge. Peter wrote, "Grow in grace and knowledge of our Lord and Savior Jesus Christ" (2 Pet. 3:18). We have an example of this in the case of Jesus, for it is written of him: "And the child grew and became strong; he was filled with wisdom, and the grace of God was upon him" (Luke 2:40). If you know Jesus as your Savior, you should never stop learning about him and what he has done for you.

3. We need to exercise the gift for serving others that God has given each of us.

We do not often think of the grace of God and the gifts of God as belonging together necessarily, but it is significant that a number of Bible passages combine the two ideas. For example, Peter wrote that each Christian "should use whatever gift he has received to serve others, faithfully administering God's grace in its various forms" (1 Pet. 4:10). In the same way, Paul wrote to the church at Ephesus, saying, "To each one of us grace has been given as Christ apportioned it" (Eph. 4:7). Therefore, when we pray that "the grace of the Lord Jesus Christ be with God's people," one thing we are praying for is that each might use the gift he has been given.

4. We need a continuing supply of grace in order to grow in grace and thus complete the work God assigns us.

Paul mentioned often how conscious he was of having received much grace to carry out his calling as an apostle. To the Romans: "Through him and for his name's sake, we received grace and apostleship to call people from among all the Gentiles to the obedience that comes from faith" (Rom. 1:5); "By the grace given me I say to every one of you . . ." (Rom. 12:3); and ". . . because of the grace God gave me" (Rom. 15:15). To the Corinthians: "By the grace God has given me, I laid a foundation as an expert builder" (1 Cor. 3:10); and "By the grace of God I am what I am, and his grace to me was not without effect. No, I worked harder than all of them—yet not I, but the grace of God that was with me" (1 Cor. 15:10). To the Ephesians: "I became a servant of this gospel by the gift of God's grace given me through the working of his power. Although I am less than the least of all God's people, this grace was given me: to preach to the Gentiles the unsearchable riches of Christ" (Eph. 3:7-8).

Paul was also aware that God gave others grace to do the work to which he had appointed them. He told the Corinthians, "God is able to make all grace abound to you, so that in all things at all times, having all that you need, you will abound in every good work" (2 Cor. 9:8). We should also have this truth in mind when we wish an abundance of "the grace of the Lord Jesus Christ" upon others.

Amen and Amen

The very last word of the very last verse of the very last book of
the Bible is *amen*. It means "firm," "faithful" or "true." When
uttered as a response to some declaration it means "so let it be."
In the New Testament *amen* is found in 127 verses, but in many
of these it occurs twice because Jesus frequently prefaced his
teaching with the repeated words, "Amen, amen, I say to you."
The King James Version translates this as "Verily, verily." Other
versions say, "Truly, truly" (New American Standard Bible), or "I
tell you the truth" (NIV). In any case, it is a declaration by Jesus
that what he is about to utter is the very truth of God.

But here is the interesting thing. In 76 verses the word *amen*
occurs at the beginning of a sentence. In 48 verses it is found at
the end. It is always God who uses the word at the beginning, and
it is always man who uses it at the end. In other words, God says,
"I solemnly affirm that what I am about to say is truthful. You
may stake your life upon it." We who hear him speak respond by
adding our amen to his saying. It means, "We believe what you
are saying and are prepared to act on it."

So do we? Do you? Can you say your amen to the doctrines
of grace we have been studying?

We have learned in these chapters that although "the law was
given through Moses; grace and truth came through Jesus
Christ" (John 1:17). Can you say amen to that? Have you found
Jesus to be the very embodiment as well as the only true source
of grace and truth? Like Peter, can you say to Jesus, "Lord, to
whom shall we go? You have the words of eternal life. We believe
and know that you are the Holy One of God" (John 6:68-69)?

We have learned in these studies that salvation is by grace
alone. "For it is by grace you have been saved, through faith—
and this not from yourselves, it is the gift of God—not by works,
so that no one can boast" (Eph. 2:8-9). Have you said your amen

to that? Have you acknowledged that you have nothing to offer God in your natural, sinful state and that you can never be saved by your own good works or good intentions, that salvation is by grace alone? That is the very minimum of belief to be a Christian. It is the place to start if you have never done so earlier.

We have seen that justification also comes by the grace of God alone because "there is no difference, for all have sinned and fall short of the glory of God, and are justified freely by his grace through the redemption that came by Christ Jesus" (Rom. 3:22-24).

We have seen that grace has brought us into a new standing before God (Rom. 5:2), that grace is triumphant and abounding (Rom. 5:20-21), that we can be strong in grace (2 Tim. 2:1), that the grace of God will be sufficient for us regardless of any specific burdens or hardships we may be given to bear by God (2 Cor. 12:9), that we may approach the throne of God's grace confidently in prayer (Heb. 4:16), and that "the God of all grace, who called you to his eternal glory in Christ, after you have suffered a little while, will himself restore you and make you strong, firm and steadfast" (1 Pet. 5:10). These are all great truths, the very greatest of truths. Can you say your amen to them?

God has already spoken his amen. He tells you that you can count on his amazing grace now and always. Let your heart echo, "Amen and amen."

SUBJECT INDEX

Scripture Index

Cassette tapes of this study on *Glory of God's Grace*
are available by calling or writing:

ALLIANCE
OF CONFESSING EVANGELICALS

1716 Spruce Street • Philadelphia, Pennsylvania 19103
215·546·3696

Also by James Montgomery Boice

Christ's Call to Discipleship

Discover what it means to live a life of true discipleship—recognizing Christ's dominion not only as Savior but also as Lord.

Christ's Call to Discipleship describes total commitment as it explores the meaning, path, cost, and rewards of being a true disciple. As Dr. Boice asserts in the preface, "I believe that if America could produce a generation of Christians who genuinely affirm and live by these teachings, that generation by the power of God could transform the world."

0-8254-2074-1   168 pages   paperback

Also by James Montgomery Boice

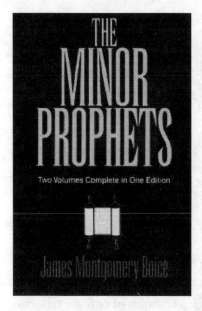

The Minor Prophets
Two Volumes Complete in One Edition

This two-volumes-in-one commentary on the Minor Prophets provides pastors, Sunday school teachers, and lay readers with an insightful guide to the backgrounds and prophetic messages of twelve key Old Testament books. Dr. Boice applies his thorough knowledge of scholarship to the Scripture text without losing sight of the spiritual truths and personal applications that permeate the prophetic writings.

"Few portions of Scripture have been so challenging to me as the Minor Prophets. It is not that they are hard to interpret. . . . Rather it is because they speak so directly and powerfully to present sins."
　　　　　　—James Montgomery Boice, from the Preface

0-8254-2148-9　　　　544 pages　　　paperback

Also by James Montgomery Boice

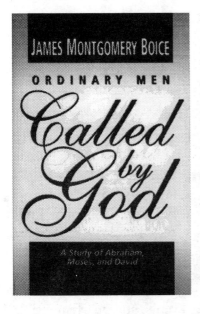

Ordinary Men Called by God
A Study of Abraham, Moses, and David

Abraham never expected to be the father of a great nation. Moses never expected to be the great leader of a special people. David never expected to be Israel's greatest king. But God called these ordinary men to become extraordinary heroes of faith and accomplishment. Their examples of courage, faithfulness, and humility give practical lessons in Christian living and service to God.

"Before God each of these men was great primarily because he humbled himself," observes Boice. "If each reader of this book could learn this lesson and practice it, the impact upon our homes, churches, businesses, and nation would be immeasurable."

0-8254-2075-x   144 pages   paperback

Also by James Montgomery Boice

Standing on the Rock
Upholding Biblical Authority in a Secular Age

"I have seen many human theories and many popular fads come and go," Boice observes in the Preface. "But the Word of God remains like a rock in the midst of raging storms, treacherous offshore currents, and nearly invisible quicksands."

Boice presents overwhelming evidence that, not only has God spoken through His Word, but He has communicated a trustworthy and authoritative message. It is a message without error and one that remains sufficient in every way for our salvation.

0-8254-2073-3   200 pages   paperback